The Paradox of a Mortal Mind

I0528879

Michael Drake

Contents

Dedication

To Joe.

Joe was a magnet for positivity and always gave back. His loss is felt by many. Thank you for your friendship and for teaching us that—above all else—time is our most valuable asset.

To Fred.

A guiding light for our family sharing both a strong faith and a love for reading. Thank you for your guidance and your love. You are missed.

To my wife.

Your unwavering love and support have been my foundation throughout this journey. Thank you for helping me become a better version of myself.

And to my daughter—my why—you bring meaning to every moment.

Acknowledgments

No book is ever finished in complete isolation, and this book is no exception.

To the modern-day intellects, ancient stoics and philosophers who helped shape our thoughts and feelings around mortality. It isn't easy to make sense of the unknown. Your efforts, thoughts and written texts have left a lasting impact on me and countless others.

To the modern writers and thinkers about our place in the world. Your knowledge and insights continue to shape our perspectives on mortality. I hope to add a small piece to that collective. I've compiled my own reading list at the end of this book.

To Mike—your wealth of knowledge and literary prowess were invaluable in shaping this work. Your insights made *The Paradox of a Mortal Mind* not just a book but a reflection of something deeper. Thank you for your wisdom, patience and the generosity of your time.

To Tyler—thank you for helping me step back and see this book from a broader perspective. Your ability to shift the lens and challenge my thinking ensured that this work not only feels right today but, I hope, will still feel right years from now.

And to my daughter—my why. Everything I create, I create with you in mind.

This is for you.

Foreword

Dear Reader,

I want to start by acknowledging the difficult nature of this topic. It's not easy to talk about death. It's painful, and that pain is real. If you've picked up this book, I'm willing to bet you've experienced a painful loss of your own—of a family member, a member of your work community, a close friend or even a family pet. That lingering ache can feel overwhelming at times. I've felt it, too, and so has every other reader in this community. We're all in this together and we've all struggled with these thoughts just like you.

But here's the harsh truth about death—no matter how uncomfortable or painful it may be, death is an undeniable part of life—It completes the circle. We can't escape it, no matter how much we try. That's reality.

Think about it—every living thing, from the smallest plant to the largest animal, will eventually reach the end of its journey. And yes, that includes us. Yet, in the fast-paced world we live in, with full schedules and constant distractions, we often choose to ignore this truth. We live as though we have an endless supply of time. The reality, however, is that we don't.

Acknowledging one's death may sound dark or bleak at first, but it's not meant to be. In fact, I'm making the argument that accepting our mortality is one of the most freeing realizations we can have. It's all about perspective.

This book is an attempt to see the paradox in death. I know it's counterintuitive to think of death as a positive thing, but when we acknowledge the inevitability of it, we *release control* and we become free to live a life filled with purpose, passion and perspective. We release the fear and the sadness that encompasses death.

When we concede that our time on earth is finite, we begin to give it more value. The trivial worries, the endless distractions and the grudges we've held onto for years—they fade into the background. What remains are the things that matter: meaningful relationships, experiences and memories with the people we love and the legacy we'll leave behind.

"It's not that life is short, but that we waste much of it."

This wisdom is from Seneca, the great Stoic philosopher. It reminds us that our lives aren't as brief as they seem; rather, they're often spent on things that don't truly matter. Seneca's reflections on time compel us to focus on what makes life truly meaningful.

The pages in this book are an invitation to explore these ideas around your mortality together. It's not about focusing on the end of your life but about learning how to live more fully in the present moment. Developing the mindset to fill your remaining days with meaning and purpose.

Along the way, I'll share with you what I've learned—from my own experiences, the knowledge I've gained from all the writers in my reading list and from the wisdom of those who came before us. I'll offer you tools, ancient perspectives and modern insights to help you develop a healthier relationship with mortality, not as something to fear but as a guide toward a more intentional, purposeful life.

Full disclosure: I'm not an expert on death. I hold no degrees in this field, nor do I speak about it in front of thousands of people. I'm just a regular person grappling with the same questions you are. I'm not here to give you all the answers because I don't have them. But I do believe that contemplating these age-old questions can help us all live better, more intentional lives. I'm just continuing a conversation that has challenged and inspired intellectuals and philosophers for generations.

The concept of facing and acknowledging your own mortality has been around for centuries. The Stoics practiced something called **memento mori,** which means "**Remember you must die.**" They didn't dwell on death out of morbid curiosity; they used it as a tool to live more fully.

Marcus Aurelius (121-180 AD), the Roman emperor and Stoic philosopher, would regularly meditate on death to keep his priorities straight. His advice was simple yet profound:

"You could leave life right now.

Let that determine what you do and say and think."

The Stoics also practiced **memento vivere**, which means "**Remember you must live.**" This helps us appreciate that our time here on earth is short and we must make the most of it by living with intention and purpose. Surrounding ourselves with people who inspire us and lift us up.

As you read, I encourage you to approach this journey with an open heart. You don't need to have everything figured out—I certainly don't, and none of us do. Instead, let's explore life's biggest questions together with honesty and compassion.

Thank you for being here and for wading into these deep waters with me. My aspiration for this book is to allow you to *slow down* and really think about your life and its meaning. We are all leaving a legacy whether you like it or not. What legacy will you leave behind?

By the end of this book, my hope is that you walk away with a renewed sense of purpose, a clearer understanding of what matters most to you and a renewed appreciation for the time you have left.

In the end, the time you have left with your loved ones is what truly matters.

With empathy and gratitude,

Michael

Lessons from the Workshop

Some of my most cherished memories are of learning woodworking from my grandfather. As a young boy, I looked up to him with a sense of awe and admiration, seeing him not just as a man who worked hard for his family but as someone with a quiet mastery of his craft. He was a hero to me through my 6-year-old eyes.

He had a workshop that was tucked away in the basement of his modest bungalow. It was a small, cluttered space that felt like a world of its own. The six-hour drive was always worth it. We did it multiple times per year! We'd pass the same Good Year warehouse and my sister would call it "bonne année." As soon as we arrived, I'd ask my grandfather what he was building next—and with a sly look on his face, we'd make our way down to the workshop.

Stepping inside, I was always hit with the rich smell of freshly cut wood and sawdust—a scent that I'll forever associate with him. The rhythmic clinking of his tools echoed in the background, mingling with the soft hum of an old radio that seemed to play timeless tunes and, of course, the habs game on a Saturday night. It was as if the space itself was suspended in time. To my young eyes, the place felt magical, like the workshop of a master craftsman, which, in many ways, it was.

At the time, I was too small to fully understand the depth of what he was teaching me in that workshop, but somehow I knew it was important. He didn't just show me how to cut or sand wood—he was patient, always explaining each step with care.

I remember sitting on a stool, my legs swinging freely as I watched him work, completely mesmerised by the way his hands moved with such precision and purpose. He had a way of making everything look easy, and I'd marvel at how a rough block of wood could be transformed into something beautiful under his guidance.

In many ways, those early lessons stayed with me long after I grew too tall for that little stool in the corner. In retrospect, my grandfather wasn't just showing me how to work with wood; he was showing me how to build a life with integrity, love and meaning. And through the eyes of a young boy, he was nothing short of a hero.

My grandfather was born in Ireland in 1917, near the end of World War I, a time when the country was grappling with severe economic hardships. Ireland, like much of the world, was reeling from the devastation of war. A few short years later, the Great Depression hit, further intensifying the struggles of daily life. Jobs were scarce, poverty was widespread, and financial hardship was a constant reality for many families, including his.

Time passed, and he matured into a young man trying to find his way in the world. Life wasn't easy, but my grandfather's determination to support his family was unwavering. No matter how tough things got, he always put the needs of his loved ones above his own, embodying a quiet strength that defined him.

He needed work badly and made the decision to move him and my grandmother to London in 1939 to help with the war effort—working as a 22-year-old firefighter and collecting scrap metal for the British Army. Scrap metal was abundant after the German bombs destroyed the city in the summer of 1940.

Eventually, seeking better opportunities, my grandfather made the bold decision to move his wife and three children—including my mother—to Canada. The transition was hard; leaving behind the familiarity of Ireland and facing the challenges of a new country wasn't easy. But he took it on with the same determination he had always shown, working tirelessly to build a better life for his family.

———--------------------

My grandfather was a master storyteller. As a young boy, I soaked it all up. As we shaped pieces of wood into something beautiful and useful, he would share stories about his life, blending wisdom with humour, teaching me far more than just the mechanics of using a chisel or reading the grain of a board. His stories were always engaging and filled with lessons about love, courage, failure and joy. I was mesmerized by the stories of the war and his journey to Canada.

But it wasn't until he began to speak about his own mortality that I understood how deeply he had contemplated the meaning of it all. He had a way of speaking about death that was different than most people. He did it without fear, hesitation or sadness. He accepted it as a natural part of life, something as certain and real as the wood we shaped together.

"One day," as he stared me in the eye, "You'll have to use these tools yourself. I won't be here forever." Later, I realised he wasn't just talking about woodworking tools. He was talking about the lessons and skills he was teaching me along the way. He was helping me develop the tools for myself to live a fulfilling life.

My grandfather never coddled me. Even when I was a young boy, he always set high expectations, believing in what I could achieve and pushing me to rise to any challenge. "You see, Michael," he'd say, sanding down a rough edge, "Knowing your time is limited makes every moment more precious. It forces you to find purpose in every action and to not waste a second on things that don't matter."

He believed that the secret to a meaningful life lay in accepting death—not as something to be dreaded or feared, but as a reminder that our time here is finite. He knew better than most that time is our most valuable asset, far more precious than money or possessions. *"Memento Mori,"* he'd often whisper to me like some wise old philosopher. I had absolutely no idea what that meant at the time and just nodded, thinking it was another one of his mysterious grandpa sayings, like when he'd tell me to "Stop growing up so fast"—as if I had any control over that!

My grandfather had a quiet way of teaching, never lecturing, just living his truth and letting me observe. He took me to the local church to help with a fundraiser. I remember being curious about the work and wondering how much he got paid for it. "Getting paid isn't important," he told me. "Helping people less fortunate is the right thing to do, and it leaves a legacy." That idea stuck with me, but it didn't fully hit home until years later. I had absolutely no idea what a legacy was.

He didn't feel the pressure to chase wealth or status. Instead, he focused on what truly mattered – family, friends, community, passion and living each day with purpose. He never hurried through life or treated time as if it were an endless resource. To him, every moment was an opportunity to do something meaningful, whether that was helping at the local church, shaping pieces of wood into something special or spending time with the people he loved.

In those moments with my grandfather, I realised that his relationship with his mortality was not one of resignation but of empowerment. By accepting the inevitability of his own death, he lived each day with a clarity and purpose that I found inspiring. His stories and perspective shaped my understanding of life and death, teaching me that by facing my own mortality, I would learn to live more fully and meaningfully.

—---

When my grandfather passed away, I was just 10 years old. It was just before Christmas that year and the entire family was devastated. I remember crying by myself in his empty workshop—staring at all the tools so neatly organized. This time, however, there was no radio playing in the background.

The loss hurt deeply and I was sad. But over time, the wound began to heal. I moved forward, as people do, making friends, chasing experiences, and exploring life's pleasures. I developed into a happy teenager enjoying all the new experiences one does.

As the years went by, the pace of life seemed to pick up. I went away to school and learned how to take care of myself without the safety net of my parents. I graduated and started a career, only to realise that it wasn't for me. I met my beautiful wife and we built a life together. Eventually, we were blessed with our amazing daughter. The days blurred into weeks, the weeks into years, and I became caught up in the speed of life—the hustle, the bustle, the constant chase to do more, to be more.

I made new friends, explored the world and experienced the many pleasures life has to offer. I chased new opportunities, sought acceptance from my peers, started a side hustle and burnt the candle at both ends on numerous occasions. All the while, the lessons I had learned from my grandfather receded further and further into the background.

For so many years, I found myself caught in the whirlwind of life: shouldering the responsibility of providing for my family and raising our wonderful daughter to be kind-hearted and full of passion. All while trying to build a career that felt both meaningful and fulfilling. It was a lot to carry, and I know many of you readers are doing the same—pouring your heart and soul into what matters most to you.

To anyone reading this who is working tirelessly for the ones you love, I see you, and I want you to know that what you're doing is deeply noble and incredibly important.

But sometimes, no matter how hard you work or how much you try to keep everything balanced, life throws you an unexpected curveball. Sometimes, life hits you hard right when you're least prepared. You might face a sudden health scare, or someone you love could end up in the hospital. And in the worst moments, you might lose someone far too soon, leaving you grappling with the unfairness of it all. These moments provide a stark reminder of just how fragile life is, and they force us to pause and rethink everything.

I recently experienced one of those devastating curveballs firsthand. I lost a friend to cancer. He was my age, and our daughters were the same age—a parallel that pierced my heart far more deeply than I ever could have imagined.

Over the years, I've attended many funerals, but this one was profoundly different. The tears were rolling down my face uncontrollably. It wasn't just the loss of a friend; it felt like the loss of something essential, a brutal reminder of how fragile life truly is.

And as much as I hate to admit it, selfish thoughts crept into my mind. What if it had been me? What would my wife do? How would my daughter cope? Have I left a meaningful impact? During the funeral, I kept looking at his daughter—a seven-year-old—and I was wondering what she was thinking, what she was feeling. The reality of it all hit me like a ton of bricks, and I couldn't help but imagine my family trying to navigate a world without me in it. It was a sobering, terrifying thought that lingered long after the funeral.

As the days and weeks passed after the funeral, memories of my grandfather began to resurface, often at the most unexpected times. Little moments from my childhood—his voice, his laughter, the quiet wisdom he'd share when we sat together—kept coming back to me even though it's been over 33 years since his passing. I found myself frantically journaling these memories, afraid that if I didn't write them down, they might fade away for good.

His words, long tucked away in the corners of my mind, began to resound with a new clarity. My grandfather had always believed that death, while inevitable, could serve as a powerful motivator—a reminder to live with intention and to embrace life fully. His wisdom, once so clear but then clouded by the busyness of life, returned to me now, sharpened by the recent loss of my friend. It was as though this grief brought my grandfather's lessons back into focus, urging me to see life through his eyes again.

With my friend's passing, something profound shifted inside me. It was as if a veil had been lifted, and I began seeing life with a new sense of urgency and clarity. I've become more intentional in my thoughts, more conscious of my own mortality, and surprisingly, more accepting of it. Instead of pushing away the inevitable or pretending that time is

limitless, I've started to embrace the reality that life is finite—
and that's exactly what gives it meaning.

I'm no longer as easily swept up in the endless rush of day-to-day life. I've become more selective with my time and more careful about how I spend it—and with whom I share it. Whether it's choosing to invest in deeper, more meaningful relationships or simply carving out moments of quiet reflection, I've found myself focusing on what truly matters. This shift has given me the freedom to live with a greater sense of purpose, allowing me to prioritize what feeds my soul rather than what drains it.

As I move forward in life, I'm drawn to the lessons this journey has brought to light. I've begun to embrace and live by the principles of this book. To actively accept the inevitability of my death—not as something to fear but as a guide that helps me make the most of the present moment. To live more authentically toward my ever-evolving purpose, to embody gratitude toward the meaningful relationships in my life and to leave a legacy I'm proud of.

My hope is that it does the same for you.

Your Journey Starts Here

As we begin this journey together, please know that what follows may be challenging to read. Yet, it's shared with the deepest compassion and respect for where you are in your life. This part of the path may feel difficult, even uncomfortable, but it's intended to be a guiding light—a moment to help you slow down, reflect on where you are and grow into who you're meant to be.

Welcoming this experience into your own life can lead to a profound sense of understanding, self-compassion and growth. Remember, you're not alone, and every step forward, even the hard ones, are steps towards something meaningful and transformative.

Let's be honest with each other—embracing our mortality may be the hardest thing you've ever done! Seriously! It's uncomfortable and sometimes even a bit scary. For many of us, thinking about death brings up a deep, instinctive fear, one that we often try to push aside or avoid altogether. After all, death is the great unknown, the one thing none of us can fully understand or control.

We live in a culture that often encourages us to ignore it, to keep busy and to focus on anything but the inevitable. And yet, no matter how much we try to distract ourselves, the fear of death lingers beneath the surface. And that fear is legitimate.

Death also forces us to confront the impermanence of everything around us. Loved ones, relationships, achievements, even our sense of self—*all of it is temporary*.

But here's the thing: just like that "check engine" light on your dashboard, avoiding these fears doesn't make them go away. In fact, the more we suppress them, the more power they hold over us (and it produces a more expensive mechanic bill). That's the funny thing about fear: the only way to move past it is to face it head-on.

These fears of death can have a ripple effect on the lives of our loved ones. We can transfer those fears to our children and grandchildren; they can trap us in cycles of anxiety or cause us to cling to things that no longer serve us—whether that's material possessions, relationships or even an outdated sense of identity.

Here's the paradox of a mortal mind: by acknowledging the reality of our own death—by facing the fear—*we actually free ourselves*. We stop being paralyzed by the fear of the unknown, and instead, we start to focus on what <u>we can control</u>—how we live today, how we love, how we spend our time and how we create meaning—right now. When we confront our fears head-on, we shift the focus away from what we're losing and toward what we have right now, in this very moment.

"The present moment is the only time over which we have dominion."

Thich Nhat Hanh

We stop taking things for granted. We cherish the small, everyday moments more deeply. We become more intentional with our time, more engaged with the people we care about and more willing to follow our passions and dreams. In short, we live with a renewed sense of purpose because we understand that our time is limited and we want to make the most of it.

Embracing mortality is scary, it's uncomfortable, and, let's be honest, it's not exactly a conversation starter at parties. But it's also surprisingly empowering. It pushes us to see life from a new angle, focus on what truly matters and let go of all the crap that is holding us back. This journey isn't about banishing fear; it's about transforming it into a tool that helps us live with more freedom, courage and clarity.

In the pages that follow, we'll explore how to make this mindset shift—how to confront the legitimate fears of death and uncertainty in a way that allows us to live more purposefully, more mindfully and with a greater sense of peace. This journey is about finding liberation, not in denying death, but in learning to embrace it as a natural part of life. In doing so, we unlock the key to living with more joy, resilience and meaning.

So, while the fear of death is real and understandable, it doesn't have to hold you back. Together, we'll walk through those fears and come out the other side with a greater appreciation for the preciousness of life. And in embracing our mortality, we'll discover a new way to live—one that is rich with intention, connection and purpose.

This book is your companion on that journey. Together, we'll break through the barriers that keep us from living fully so you can experience life not just as something that happens *to* you but as something you actively shape.

Acceptance isn't resignation—it's empowerment. It's like flipping a switch in your mind. Suddenly, you realize that every moment is an opportunity. Living with purpose is a choice you can make every single day. This shift in thinking can be liberating because, instead of running away from the reality of life's impermanence, you learn to walk alongside it, using it as a motivator to live with intention.

So, I invite you to slow down and take a deep breath. This isn't an end—it's the beginning of a new way of thinking. Together, we'll reframe how we look at life and mortality, making sure every day counts.

Accepting death isn't about giving up; it's about waking up.

Memento Mori

Remember, you must die.

Chapter 1
Facing the Fear of Death

"It is not death that a man should fear,

but he should fear never beginning to live."

Marcus Aurelius

This book isn't for everyone. Changing your perspective on life and making the most of your existence isn't something you just breeze through in one afternoon. This isn't a book about following a simple, ten-step guide either. It's about *perspective* and *willingness*—about how you view your place in the world and whether you're ready to do something about it. This requires facing realities that may make us feel vulnerable or even uncomfortable, and that's okay! Life begins at the end of your comfort zone.

Gary John Bishop wrote about perspective and willingness in his book "Unf*ck Yourself." Amazing read. I highly recommend it. Bishop's message is that your perspective creates your reality, and your willingness determines whether you change it.

If you're the type who's ready to step out of 'autopilot' and actively shape your perspective on how you live and value your time, then you're in the right place. If not, there is no harm in giving this a go anyway—you might just surprise yourself.

Perspective

Perspective, which is just a fancy word for how we look at things, is about how we interpret our day-to-day moments, our relationships and our place in the world. Perspective allows us to acknowledge our relative insignificance in the world and to see that the time we have is both fleeting and precious, not just something that stretches out endlessly ahead of us.

Shifting this perspective may mean acknowledging things we often ignore or refuse to accept, like the fact that 100 years from now, the work we did, the houses we built and even the people we loved will likely be forgotten. This is no slight against you or the work you've done in your life—it's a fact.

All of it is temporary.

Willingness

Willingness is that hard-to-define commitment not to just think about these concepts but to *do something* with it. It's about making an intentional choice to take action. Whether that means dedicating more time to relationships, pursuing long-held dreams, leaving a legacy for your loved ones, or simply deciding to value the moment you're in. This book is about developing a new way of thinking—but at the end of the day, it's up to you to use that awareness to make conscious choices.

Each of us is a small yet essential part of a greater whole. From the vastness of the universe to the intricacies of human relationships, our lives are interconnected in ways we often overlook. Shifting how we see ourselves in this web of life can be profoundly transformative, but it isn't always easy.

It's natural for humans to fear death. After all, our survival instincts are hardwired to avoid it at all costs. For centuries, our main focus every day was simply to survive. Humans continually created ways to live longer and create safer environments for their families.

Fearing death doesn't mean we should shy away from thinking about it. The only way I know to overcome fear is to face it head-on. Fear of rollercoasters? Keep on avoiding them and see if the fear goes away. You and I both know the only way to overcome that fear is to strap in and ride that roller coaster!

Changing our *perspective*—especially on something as fundamental as life and death—takes effort, openness and a *willingness* to step outside our comfort zone. When we stop seeing death as just an end and start viewing it as part of the cycle of life, we open ourselves up to living more fully. It's in this shift that we find a new way to approach our lives with intention, gratitude and a deeper sense of purpose.

It's understandable to cling to familiar ways of thinking, especially when confronting fears as deep as mortality. We often steer clear of what unsettles us, preferring the safety of our established beliefs. But this avoidance, while comforting at the moment, can hold us back from the growth and understanding that come from facing life's harder truths. By challenging ourselves to explore new perspectives, we open up the possibility for greater peace and a richer, more meaningful experience of life. Even the greatest minds to ever walk this earth didn't have it all figured out when they reached the end of their journey.

Embracing a new perspective, although challenging, is worth the effort because it opens the door to greater insight and a deeper sense of connection to the world around us. We allow ourselves the opportunity to find peace in unexpected places, to reframe our fears and to approach life with renewed appreciation.

The fact that you've picked up this book tells me that you're ready (and willing) to challenge yourself. This book invites you to explore these shifts in perspective with me. It's not about denying the realities of life or death but about understanding them in a way that enriches our experience of being alive. By taking the time to reflect on our place in the grander scheme of things and accepting the ebb and flow of existence, we begin to see that *life's beauty often lies in its impermanence.*

The fear of death is not a weakness; it's a natural part of being alive, woven into our survival instinct, pushing us to protect and preserve ourselves. In fact, fearing death is as universal as life itself.

Throughout history, countless cultures, philosophies and religions have sought to explain or cope with death. From ancient myths about the afterlife to modern discussions of consciousness and legacy, our desire to understand and make peace with death demonstrates how deeply it affects us.

The fear of death touches everyone at some point, whether in moments of personal reflection, illness or the loss of a loved one. Acknowledging this fear, instead of denying or suppressing it, can be the first step toward finding meaning and comfort in life itself.

Look at the natural world around you for comfort. In nature, life and death are intertwined; a fallen tree becomes nutrients for new saplings, and flowers that wither away in winter make way for fresh buds in spring. Much like nature, we are both shaped by the world we inhabit and, in our own way, add to the world's ongoing story.

However, humans have a unique gift. We have a remarkable awareness not just of our surroundings but also of our unique place within them. We look up at the stars and feel awe, wonder, and, now and then, a bit of existential curiosity. We notice the passing of time, we reflect on it, and we ask ourselves big questions about our purpose and the impact we want to make.

We're not only aware of our own experiences, but also of the larger tapestry of life, we're part of. And while that might make us the only species prone to midlife crises, existential spirals, or even that urge to drop everything and move to a beach to "find ourselves," it does give us one massive advantage: the chance to actually shape our lives with intention.

Unlike humans, animals in the wild aren't lying awake, wondering what it all means. A lion isn't busy fretting about its last roar. You won't see a monkey pausing in a tree, pondering if it's making the most of its days. And that goldfish in its bowl? Blissfully unaware of concepts like "mortality" or "bucket lists."

Humans are special. We have been gifted with the capacity for introspection, for asking the big questions—why are we here? How will I be remembered after I'm gone? And what should we do with our time? And, of course, we're equally prone to pondering the little questions, too, like why every washing machine seems determined to leave us with a single, unmatched sock. It's this curiosity that makes us human, this ability to consider not just what we do but what it all means.

This awareness of our place in the world is both a privilege and a responsibility. As Peter Parker's Uncle Ben so wisely said, "With great power comes great responsibility." Sure, he was talking about superpowers, but honestly, self-awareness might just be *our* version of it—minus the ability to swing from buildings, of course.

This awareness is a gift—it allows us to live with intention, purpose and gratitude. Unlike other creatures, we have the ability to reflect, make choices and shape our lives in meaningful ways. We should be grateful for this gift, as it gives us a chance to not only appreciate the present moment but also to live in a way that truly matters, leaving behind a legacy of love, wisdom and connection.

After all, we have the power to reflect on our existence, actively shape our choices and make the most of the time we have. It's a pretty big deal! And yes, this means we carry a little extra "responsibility" baggage. But with this unique human gift, we get to live with purpose. Or at least try not to waste too much time wondering where all the matching socks went.

Here's a quick reality check: talking about death is uncomfortable for most of us! Many of us put it off or avoid the topic entirely as if by dodging it, we can somehow outwit it. Trust me, I was right there, sidestepping any serious thoughts on mortality like it was an awkward chore. But after recently losing a close friend, I found myself unable to brush it aside any longer.

It's important to acknowledge that this fear is *normal*. Feeling anxious or uneasy about death doesn't make you weak—it makes you human. But here's the thing: we're all in the same boat, no exceptions. Every single one of us is on this wild ride with the same destination. Take comfort with the people around you, and why not embrace it with a little humor and grace along the way?

This book is a personal example of me confronting this universal fear. By writing down my thoughts and reflections, I've been able to explore and better understand my own feelings about death—its uncertainty, its inevitability and the ways in which it shapes our lives. Writing these thoughts out on paper has not only been therapeutic for me, but it has also allowed me to engage with the fear head-on, transforming something overwhelming into something that feels more tangible and manageable.

In sharing this, I hope to extend that same therapeutic process to you. Communicating our fears—whether it's death or any other deeply ingrained anxiety—has the power to bring clarity and calm. Just as it has helped me begin to come to terms with death, it can offer you the space to reflect, heal and perhaps see your own life with a new sense of appreciation.

In the end, it doesn't matter where you were born, the color of your skin, your height, your accent, your faith, your pronouns or your preferences. None of this changes this universal fact. No amount of kale, marathon medals, meditation apps or VIP status will change our shared fate. We're all ending up at the same finish line. And maybe that's the beauty of it!

Understanding the Psychology of Death

I've been diving into the world of psychology for the last couple of years, and I stumbled across this fascinating concept called "mortality salience." Sounds fancy, right? Basically, it's a term psychologists use to describe that moment when we become super aware that, yup, we're going to die one day. Fun, huh? But here's the kicker: mortality salience has a huge impact on how we think and behave in our lives today.

It turns out that being reminded of our mortality can be the ultimate motivator. Knowing that time's ticking makes us do all sorts of things—some awesome, like chasing our dreams or telling people we love them. Others, well, let's just say questionable—like impulse-buying that ridiculous gadget you never needed or sky-diving after seeing an ad in the classifieds. It's like having a constant clock in the back of our minds, nudging us to act before our time runs out.

For some, mortality salience pushes them to live more fully, to appreciate each moment, and to focus on what really matters. For others, it triggers a "YOLO" spiral of questionable choices. But hey, no judgment—we're all just trying to navigate this whole "life" thing!

While I'm definitely not a psychology expert, I'm starting to see how embracing this idea of mortality salience can actually be a powerful tool. Instead of letting it freak us out, maybe we can use it as a gentle reminder to stop sweating the small stuff, spend our remaining days with the people we love, and figure out what inspires us—before the clock runs out.

Mortality Salience stems from a broader concept called Terror Management Theory (TMT)—yes, that's a real thing, and not a spooky movie title—the fear of death is such a powerful force that it drives humans to seek self-preservation, personal achievement and legacy. Basically, we're all trying to make our mark on the world so we don't just fade away—like that questionable high school haircut we'd all rather forget. Thank goodness I was in high school before social media!

The theory suggests that because we know our time is limited, we're constantly trying to find ways to *feel* immortal— whether it's through having lots of kids, writing a book (hmm—this makes me think), building a business, joining a religion or even just making sure our Instagram feed is on point.

TMT says we humans are in a lifelong game of "Let's Beat Death," where we think things like, If I can just win this award, get that promotion, or become a meme sensation, then maybe, just maybe, I'll live on forever! Spoiler alert: we won't. But hey, that doesn't stop us from trying!

What's funny (and a little ridiculous) is that our quest for immortality doesn't always lead to deep, meaningful achievements. Sometimes, it leads to spending three hours perfecting a TikTok dance just to get a few likes. Or buying a car so flashy that your neighbors start wearing sunglasses just to check the mail. Because, apparently, if we can't physically stick around forever, we might as well be remembered for something fabulous.

In the end, TMT is like life's cheeky little reminder that our fear of death can push us to do some truly amazing things—and, let's be real, some pretty weird things, too. But hey, as long as we're chasing meaning and laughing along the way, we're winning the game, right?

Fearing death can lead to both positive and negative behaviors. You may strive to accomplish great things, form meaningful relationships and live authentically. Conversely, the fear of mortality can lead to fear-based decision-making, overconsumption or clinging to unhealthy relationships and ideologies.

So, here's where you're going to have to pick a side: Some of you will strive for greatness, nurture meaningful relationships and leave behind a legacy. You will be open to a new *perspective* and have the *willingness* to act on it. You'll be the ones who embrace mortality as a motivator to live ethically and fully.

On the flip side, some of you might fall into the trap of making fear-based decisions, holding onto things that no longer serve you or maxing out your credit cards, trying to fill the void.

So, which side are you on? Are you willing to channel your mortality into something meaningful, nurturing connections and creating a legacy? Or are you content to coast through life, letting it spiral into doom scrolling and impulse buys?

The key is all about perspective and willingness—are you ready to make meaningful changes, or are you just stubborn enough to keep strolling down the same dead-end street?

"If you want a better life, you have to commit to doing what it takes, even when it's hard."

Gary John Bishop

Reframing Death as a Motivator

Okay, we've established that fearing the inevitability of death is normal. But instead of viewing death as something to dread, it can actually be a *motivator*—a reminder to live with intention.

When we embrace the reality of death, it can inspire us to live more fully, take meaningful and calculated risks and focus on what truly matters. By seeing death not as an impending end but as a tool to sharpen our priorities and define our legacy, we can turn fear into *purpose*.

Philosophies like *memento mori and memento vivere*, practiced by Stoics, remind us that contemplating death makes life richer, encouraging us to value the time we have. Knowing that our time is finite, we can stop procrastinating, avoid trivial pursuits and make decisions that bring us fulfillment.

My grandfather exemplified this philosophy in his day-to-day life. He never spoke of his mortality with fear. He was brave in the face of it. By embracing his mortality, he unlocked the potential to make the most of every moment and allowed him the grace to build a lasting legacy.

"The purpose of life is not to be happy. It is to be useful, to be honorable, to be compassionate, to have it make some difference that you have lived and lived well."

Ralph Waldo Emerson

Imagine your life as a story, and you are the hero. Every decision you make, every interaction you have, every goal you set—it's all part of the unfolding narrative. The fear of death doesn't hold you back; instead, it propels you forward. You become the hero in your own story by the decisions you make. With each passing day, you're given the opportunity to live with more intention, more love and more focus on what truly matters.

This book is here to help break down that self-imposed barrier of fear and silence we often place around death. It's time to talk about it openly, to embrace it not as an end but as a natural part of life's journey. Just another point in the cycle of life.

By embracing death, we can celebrate the beauty of a life well lived. We can shift our focus from fearing the unknown to making the most of every moment we have, creating memories and leaving a legacy that will carry on through the generations that follow.

"Remembering that you are going to die is the best way I know to avoid the trap of thinking you have something to lose. You are already naked. There is no reason not to follow your heart."

Steve Jobs

Let's embrace the idea that our lives can have a ripple effect far beyond our time here. By living fully and with purpose, we leave behind stories, wisdom and love that will be cherished long after we're gone. This is the legacy we leave behind.

Leaving a legacy is standard. Leaving a meaningful one is a choice.

Chapter 2
Humble Yourself

"I claim to be a simple individual liable to err like any other fellow mortal. I own, however, that I have humility enough to confess my errors and to retrace my steps."

Mahatma Gandhi

Have you ever been trapped in a conversation where the other person only talks about themselves? You know the type—the person who dominates the dialogue, going on and on about their achievements, opinions or problems without ever pausing to ask about you. The type that is in a constant state of comparison and "one-ups" you every chance they get.

Then, miraculously, you manage to get a word in, only to be interrupted by that person's version of what you're discussing. You realize, in that moment, that they're not actually listening to (or interested in) anything you're saying. They are just thinking about the next thing *they* want to say. It leaves you feeling like you're not even part of the exchange.

What you want to say is, "I'm sorry, did the middle of my sentence interrupt the beginning of yours?"

Now, imagine *being* that person.

Talking about yourself all the time doesn't teach you anything. In fact, it limits your growth. When you're busy filling the air with your own words, you're missing out on an opportunity to learn from others.

"Empty heads have long tongues"

Bruce Lee

Cultivating humility requires you to admit to yourself that you don't have all the answers. None of us do! You can always learn from others. Especially people who are older than you and have experienced more of life. Give yourself permission to save room for their thoughts and reflections. You'll be surprised at what you can absorb.

Think of a master and student relationship. The master is full of knowledge compiled from a lifetime of experiences and is happy and willing to share that knowledge with his disciples. However, if the disciple doesn't have room for that knowledge (because he thinks he has it all figured out), he cannot absorb it. Openness to learning is more valuable than possessing knowledge.

"A wise man can learn more from a foolish question than a fool can learn from a wise answer."

Bruce Lee

The trick is to surround yourself with people who make you look like you've got your act together—just by association. Ask lots of questions. Hang out with folks who are smarter, more driven and a tad wiser. Their good habits and sharp perspectives? They're like a delightful flu—highly contagious. Stick around long enough, and you'll start picking up their best qualities without even trying.

After my friend's funeral last year, I committed myself to seek out mentors to help me shape my own approach to life, drawing not only from friends and personal connections but also from the timeless wisdom of ancient Stoics, modern thinkers and admired authors. (Have a look at the reading list and the podcast list at the end of this book!).

The beauty is that mentorship is all around us—you don't need their permission or direct contact to benefit from their insights. Through books, audiobooks and podcasts, you can access a wealth of guidance whenever you want. It's never been easier to tap into all the knowledge and insights you'd ever need.

I immersed myself in the works of Stoics like Marcus Aurelius, Epictetus and Seneca, finding value in their reflections on resilience, purpose and the fleeting nature of life. Their teachings reminded me to keep perspective, focus on what I can control (and release what I can't) and embrace humility in the face of life's unpredictability.

At the same time, current thinkers and writers provide fresh insights and practical advice for navigating today's challenges, from cultivating discipline to finding joy in the journey. Authors like Ryan Holiday, Dan Sullivan, Robin Sharma, Mark Manson, Gary John Bishop, Sahil Bloom, Dan Martell, Alua Arthur and Mel Robbins have helped me shape my perspective entirely. Conversations with friends I admire also gave me perspectives on how they approach their own lives, relationships and passions.

I've found that reading and listening widely and purposefully—seeking out voices that challenge, inspire and ground me—has given me a sense of guidance as though I'm sitting in a room of wise mentors. Making time for these insights daily, whether in books, podcasts or even quick moments of reflection, has shaped the way I listen, think and operate on a daily basis.

There are wonderful podcasters out there offering a broad range of perspectives on life and its meaning. I've been diving deep into these podcasts on my drive to work, offering me perspective on a multitude of topics. Some of these podcasters include Chris Williamson, Rob Dial, Jordan Peterson, Alex Hormozi, Dan Martell, Jay Shetty, Mel Robbins and Patrick Bet-David.

Check them out for yourself and find other voices that speak directly to you and your own purpose! I encourage you to seek out this knowledge for yourself and stop pretending that you have all the answers and that your perspective is the only one that has validity. A narrow worldview will only lead to unchecked bias.

Here's another truth about mentors: people *love* being asked to be one. When you approach someone and say, "I really admire what you've done, and I'd love to learn from you," they're not going to roll their eyes or give a deep, exhausted sigh.

Nope—they'll probably light up like a Christmas tree! Why? Because being seen as a mentor is like a giant neon sign flashing, "You're awesome! Your wisdom means something!" It's flattering and affirming, and it just feels good to know that all the experience they've collected might help someone else. Plus, they get to feel like a bit of a superhero—without being bitten by a radioactive spider.

Most people who've gained some wisdom in their life are more than willing to share it, and being asked to be a mentor is validation that their journey wasn't just for their own benefit—it can now help others, too. Think about it: if someone came up to you and said, "I really admire how you handle [*insert cool skill here*], could you give me some tips?" You'd probably puff out your chest a little, right? It's the same for them.

In fact, many mentors enjoy the process of giving back. They get to relive their own struggles and successes through your journey, offering guidance they wish they had back in the day. And here's the kicker: mentors usually gain as much from the experience as you do. Helping someone else navigate life reminds them of the lessons they've learned and the wisdom they've gained and lets them refine their own thinking along the way.

So don't be shy—reach out to that person you admire. Odds are, they'll be more than happy to share their experiences, and you might just make their day in the process! It's like osmosis, but instead of absorbing water, you're soaking up success. Find the ones who are chasing after their goals, who are leveling up in life, and there's a good chance you'd start leveling up right along with them.

"Don't take criticism from people you wouldn't go to for advice."

Jim Kwik

Humility also allows you to open up to the world, to learn, and to grow in ways that pride and self-centeredness never can. It's not about downplaying your own worth but about recognizing that you don't have all the answers.

When you listen more than you speak, you create space for others to teach you. You allow for life to show you new perspectives and for relationships to deepen. And that's where real wisdom comes from—not from what you say, but from what you hear and how you apply that to your own life.

"If you're the smartest person in the room, you're in the wrong room."

Confucius

Let's also take a minute to discuss what humility *isn't*. Humility isn't pulling a "sandbagger" move, like that guy on the golf course who says, "Oh, I haven't played in *forever*," and then proceeds to nail a perfect drive down the fairway and then sticks his approach shot 12 feet from the pin. Those are fighting words in the golf world! A sandbagger pretends to be bad to hustle you for a better score, and that's not humility—that's sneaky showmanship.

Similarly, humility is not that person at a dinner party who says, "I'm not much of a cook," only to serve you a Michelin-star-worthy meal. That's not humility either; that's false modesty.

Humility definitely doesn't mean being a doormat for others to walk all over and wipe their boots. You don't have to let people trample all over you just to prove you're humble. Being humble doesn't mean shrinking away from what you're good at or pretending you're not capable. Instead, it's about having the confidence to acknowledge your strengths *without* needing to boast about them. Humility is owning your talents while lifting others up.

Think of it this way: it's like playing a round of golf and being genuinely proud of a well-executed shot, but instead of rubbing it in everyone's face, you just put your club away and say, "That one felt good," and move on. You recognize your skill without needing validation or showing off. True humility doesn't seek to impress; it seeks to connect. And in that connection, you often discover that life—just like golf—is a lot more enjoyable when you're not trying to hustle people.

True humility is more about accepting your strengths *and* your weaknesses with grace and knowing the world doesn't revolve around you. It's recognizing that while you're important, you're also just a single piece of this giant human puzzle. Think of humility as an internal GPS that keeps you from getting lost in your own ego.

Here's a quick reality check for you: You're one of almost 9 billion people on this planet. I got news for you: The chef whipping up a curry in Sri Lanka and the secretary typing away in Chile? They don't care about you at all or care about your "I'm just so busy" lifestyle, and honestly, you don't care about theirs either. But your family? They're invested. They care—a lot! So, keep things in perspective, stay humble, and maybe remember to call your mom back—better yet, make the first call.

So why is humility essential for a meaningful life? Because without it, life turns into one long episode of *The Michael Show* [insert your own name here]. You're the star, the director, and even the audience—and that gets boring really fast.

Remember Jim Carrey in *The Truman Show*? He thought he was part of a perfect little world, but in reality, he was trapped in a bubble, only seeing life from his own perspective. Without humility, we can end up living like that—thinking everything revolves around us, completely missing out on the richness of the world outside our own narrow view.

Humility pops that bubble. It lets you see the bigger picture, step outside *your* show, and realize that the world is filled with other fascinating stories. Being humble means recognizing that you don't have all the answers, and honestly? That's where the fun starts—when you open yourself up to learning, growing and seeing life from a viewpoint beyond your own. So, don't be the star of your own never-ending rerun. There are so many other shows to watch out there. Change the channel.

Memento Mori and Humility

Now, let's sprinkle some memento mori onto *your* story to keep things spicy. The phrase has been the ultimate reality check for centuries. It's a tool that prevents your head from swelling to the size of a hot air balloon.

You see, thinking about your mortality is like having that one friend who never lets you forget the time you tripped in front of your crush. It keeps you humble. When you realize that one day—sorry to break it to you—you'll no longer be around, it becomes clear that life isn't just about personal accomplishments. It's about how you live, the impact you leave behind and the relationships you built along the way.

Being aware of your own end date gives you a constant reminder: "Hey, maybe you *shouldn't* act like you're the center of the universe." It encourages gratitude for what you have, not arrogance for what you've done (or arrogance for what you've inherited). It allows you the space to listen intently and learn from people. It allows you to realize that we are all equal, ending up at the same destination.

Imagine if famous historical figures had ignored their mortality—things would have played out a little differently! We'd be talking about Alexander the Arrogant, who spent so long gazing into his own reflection that he missed the chance to conquer half the world. Or Michelangelo would have strolled into the Sistine Chapel with a paintbrush and a casual attitude, doodling his name on the ceiling like a bored high schooler: "Mike wuz here." The fact is, greatness doesn't come from assuming you'll live forever—it comes from realizing you won't. You're a single piece of a grand puzzle. We all are.

Stories of Humble Greatness

Let's dive into a few examples of people who've managed to balance greatness and humility while always keeping their mortality in mind.

Marcus Aurelius – As a Roman emperor and philosopher, Marcus Aurelius had all the power in the world, yet he was never drunk on it. His personal journal, *Meditations*, reveals a man constantly reminding himself of his mortality and the fleeting nature of life. While ruling the Roman Empire, he pondered things like: *"Soon you'll be ashes or bones. A mere name, or not even that."*

When he would come back to Rome after a great victory, the streets would be filled with loyal followers, all cheering his name. It became customary to have a person whisper in his ear, "Memento Mori." A gentle reminder that, despite his immense power and greatness, he was also mortal. Enjoy it, big guy! This party won't last forever!

Casual bedtime thoughts for an emperor, right? But this reminder had a profound purpose for him! This mortal mindset kept him grounded, fair to his people and introspective despite his immense power. It's like running the Roman Empire and remembering to call your mother-in-law on her birthday!

Nelson Mandela – After spending 27 years in prison, Mandela could have easily come out angry, bitter and ego-driven. Instead, he emerged as a leader who prioritised forgiveness over revenge and unity over division. He knew that life was short—too short to hold grudges. He also knew that yesterday could not be changed. Every day, we wake up with a choice: to be a better version of who we were yesterday. Small steps carry you long distances if you're consistent.

Even when he became president of South Africa, Mandela's humility shone through. He often downplayed his achievements, giving credit to those who fought alongside him. It's hard to imagine anyone else coming out of prison, getting elected to lead an entire country and then being like, "Yeah, it's not *just* about me."

Mother Teresa - Though she is now recognised as a saint, Mother Teresa spent her life in the gritty reality of poverty-stricken streets, choosing to serve the most marginalized. Born in Albania, she left behind the comfort of her life to live in the slums of Calcutta (now named "Kolkata" to honor the Bengali pronunciation), dedicating herself to the sick and dying.

Despite her global recognition and accolades, including a Nobel Peace Prize, Mother Teresa remained humble, frequently downplaying her own role in her work. She often said, *"I am a pencil in the hand of God,"* reminding herself and others that she was simply an instrument for something greater. Her deep faith in God and her dedication to service kept her focused on helping those who needed it most, making her life a living meditation on humility, compassion and purpose. She didn't seek praise or fame but instead lived as a quiet testament to the power of selflessness.

Keanu Reeves – Okay, okay—a more modern example, but hear me out. Despite his Hollywood fame and his uncanny ability to dodge bullets in slow motion, Keanu has a reputation for being one of the humblest guys in the business. Look him up on social media if you want! His answers to life's big questions—especially about mortality—are incredible.

> *"Every moment is precious. We're all just passing through. That's the truth."*
>
> *Keanu Reeves*

He famously rides the subway, donates large portions of his salary to charity, plays in a rock band and goes out of his way to thank his stunt crew. Maybe it's because he's faced his own share of personal tragedies that he stays so grounded.

Keanu is like the Buddha of Hollywood—constantly aware that life is fragile, unpredictable and not worth living in the clouds of ego. He probably says "Whoa" when he thinks about death, but in the most humble way possible. Take a minute and search up some of his interviews.

Stephen Colbert: "What do you think happens when we die?"

Keanu Reeves: "I know that the ones who love us will miss us."

When we look at stories of people who embodied greatness with humility, we see something special. These individuals all had every reason to be consumed by their own importance, yet they remained grounded, self-aware and in touch with their mortality.

What do all these examples have in common? They understood that life is fragile and fleeting, and because of that, they focused on serving others, not glorifying themselves. Humility is what kept them from turning their lives into *The Me Show*, and it's what made their greatness even more impactful. Humility, paired with a healthy dose of memento mori, reminds us that no matter how high we rise, gravity (and death) is always waiting.

Picture this for a moment: You've just nailed a huge presentation in front of your boss! Everyone's clapping because of your awesomeness, and you feel like you're on top of the world. But then you trip over your shoelace while leaving the stage. Bang! Right on your face. Memento mori right there, pal. Life's little way of saying, "Keep it real, champ."

So, next time you're feeling a little too self-important, just remember: one day, someone's going to have to write your eulogy, and nobody wants to write about a bragger. I mean, think about it—who wants to stand up there and say, "Well, what can I say about *Bob*? He sure loved to tell you how great he was at literally *everything*—golf, barbecuing, trivia, parallel parking, you name it."

No way! Eulogies are meant to be heartwarming and genuine, not a bullet-point resume of how many times you reminded people of your glorious *you-ness*.

So, be humble! Let people remember you for the way you made them <u>feel</u>, not how many times you mentioned your hole-in-one or that you *totally* could've gone pro if it weren't for that old knee injury.

Chapter 3
The Power of Perspective

"Every morning brings new potential, but if you dwell on the misfortunes of the day before, you tend to overlook tremendous opportunities."

Harvey Mackay

Perspective can be a lot like the Swiss Army knife—it's versatile, can get you out of a jam, and just when you think you're all set, it somehow manages to get wedged in your pocket or, even worse, mysteriously disappears right when you're reaching for it.

With the right perspective, we can find meaning in adversity, cultivate the mindset of gratitude and even feel empathetic towards people who text in all caps (YES, EVEN THEM). But let's not pretend perspective is all rainbows and deep insights. It's a double-edged sword and can be dangerous if unchecked.

On the one hand, it can open your mind to new ways of thinking, helping you realize that maybe—just maybe—you haven't been right about everything since birth. On the other hand, it can narrow your vision, making you see the world through a keyhole and reinforce those biases you pretend you don't have—like your belief that pineapple on pizza is a crime against humanity.

Perspective can be a powerful tool for self-reflection or, if wielded poorly, the world's sneakiest pair of blinders. Either way, it's there, whether you like it or not, quietly shaping your worldview. So, are you ready for the truth? Or are you still clinging to the idea that you totally "nailed" karaoke last night?

Perspective allows us to step outside of ourselves and see the world through a different set of lenses. When we experience setbacks, shifting our perspective can turn those moments into opportunities for growth. What might seem like a failure can, from another angle, be viewed as a lesson in resilience or creativity.

In relationships, perspective gives us the ability to empathise, to step into someone else's shoes and see the world through their eyes. It helps us consider their experiences and emotions, which is the key to building deeper connections and resolving conflicts.

When we widen our perspective even further, we start to see what really matters. Suddenly, the little things—those daily stressors—become temporary, fleeting and just not that important. When we develop a healthy relationship with our impermanence and put on our "mortality glasses," it's even clearer: all these problems, even the big ones, are temporary.

We are temporary.

My grandfather taught me this lesson in the simplest, most powerful way—right in his workshop. He used to say, "Measure twice, cut once." At the time, I thought it was just about woodwork and the fact that he was getting annoyed at all the pieces we had to throw away. But it was actually more than that: it was about life. He was reminding me to take a step back and think before acting. When a piece didn't fit, he didn't get mad or frustrated. He'd just smile and say, "It's just wood. There's always another piece." It was his way of showing me that mistakes, like so many of life's problems, aren't the end of the world.

In his workshop, I learned that life is about getting the cuts wrong sometimes and realizing that it's okay. After all, the sawdust can be swept up, and there's always another board. Life's imperfections, the little messes we make, are part of the process. Don't dwell on them. They are temporary; *we are temporary*. That's what makes each moment and each connection we build so valuable.

Perspective isn't just about rainbows and lollipops, either. It can also have a dark side. Serving as a powerful force in reinforcing our biases and our prejudices. Growing up in environments with limited or skewed viewpoints can cloud our understanding of realities beyond our own experiences. You simply learn what you've been taught from your family and friends. This can lead to ignorance, racism, hate and bigotry. It's important to remember that the circumstances of your upbringing are just that—circumstances. They are not your fault; they are simply the cards you've been dealt. What matters is how you play that hand.

But let's not use our upbringing as an excuse for ignorance. As you grow older and mature, *you do have the freedom of choice*. You can choose to open up your mind and learn about others and embrace the beauty in diversity. You can learn to empathize with people with a different set of beliefs or a different skin color than you. You can develop a growth mentality and strive to be better every day.

When someone's perspective is confined to only what they've been taught or experienced, they may cling to harmful stereotypes without questioning their validity. This bias can foster an "us vs. them" mentality, where differences are seen as threats instead of opportunities for learning or connection. Hate and bigotry are born when perspectives are left unchecked and unchallenged. In this way, perspective can trap us in our own mental frameworks, preventing growth and understanding. Massive wars and countless deaths are the direct result of this narrow mentality.

This is why expanding our perspective is so important. It's about consciously seeking out new experiences, learning about different cultures and accepting the fact that we are ALL human and we are no better or worse than anyone else. And— if you've absorbed anything so far in this book—we're all ending up in the same place anyway!

> *"Don't demand that things happen as you wish, but wish that they happen as they do, and you will go on well."*
>
> *Epictetus*

Ultimately, perspective is powerful because it shapes our reality—much like our Wi-Fi signal determines whether we're productive. Perspective can lift us up, helping us find meaning, compassion and maybe even the strength to survive yet another family holiday dinner. But it can also seriously mess with us. If we're not careful, perspective can turn into a carnival funhouse mirror, bending reality until suddenly we're convinced the barista who misspelled our name is part of a global conspiracy against us.

But let's make one thing abundantly clear—the key isn't just to *have* a perspective. I mean, congratulations, you're human.

You're not getting a "hero cookie" simply because you have an opinion. Perspectives come standard, like the ability to scroll endlessly through social media or procrastinate with remarkable skill. The real magic happens when you stop and think, "Hmm, is this perspective actually serving me, or am I just clinging to it like a pair of old, worn-out shoes that don't even fit anymore?"

You've got to constantly examine it, challenge it and stretch it out like yoga for your brain. You need the *willingness* (there's that word again!) to challenge yourself. Because if you don't, it's easy to get stuck, convinced that your view is the only one that matters—kind of like that one friend who swears they've figured out life because they once read half of a self-help book.

In the end, perspective is powerful. It can open doors to empathy and understanding, or it can keep you locked in a room with your worst fears. So, check your perspective often—just like you check your phone every five minutes for a notification that hasn't come. Let's look at a few perspectives you can consider:

The Spinning Rock Perspective

Let's take this whole perspective thing and stretch it as far as it can go. Ready? We're going to zoom out—*way* out. If you thought your daily problems were overwhelming, wait until you see just how small they really are in the grand scheme of things. Let's dive into this new perspective and see what happens when we look at the world from a cosmic scale. Trust me, your worries will start to feel like tiny specks of dust compared to the vastness we're about to explore!

We live on a small planet—Earth—a spinning rock floating in the galaxy. Planet Earth is part of a solar system with 7 other planets (also spinning rocks) that represent just a tiny speck in the Milky Way galaxy. (Seriously, a tiny speck).

Now, the Milky Way might sound like a cozy name, but it's far from small. Scientists estimate it contains somewhere between 100 to 400 *billion* stars (yep - each star is just like our sun). Every one of these stars is potentially orbited by planets (spinning rocks) just like ours. That's already pretty mind-blowing, right?

Don't believe me? Google it.

But hold on, it gets crazier. The Milky Way is just <u>one galaxy</u> in the universe, and while that might make you feel special, don't get too attached—because scientists estimate there could be up to *2 trillion* galaxies in the observable universe. Yeah, *trillion* with a "T," like the number of emails in your spam folder.

The number of galaxies is unfathomable. Let's give that some context for a minute—there are more <u>galaxies</u> than there are grains of sand on all the beaches on Earth. No, not just the local beach—<u>all the beaches!</u> So the next time you're walking along the shore, grab a handful of sand, let it slip through your fingers and remember: for every grain of sand falling to the ground, there's an <u>entire galaxy</u> somewhere out there.

Alright, let's say you're hopping in your spaceship, cranking it up to the speed of light—about 186,282 miles per second— which is way faster than your average commute. If you're off to visit your friend on a planet 4 light-years away (that's a cozy little distance in space terms), you'd think you'd be there in no time. Well, buckle up! Because, at light speed, you're still looking at a 4-year trip—a 4-year trip travelling at the speed of light. That's right—four years of endless space snacks, awkward silence and maybe some intergalactic podcasts to pass the time.

But really, when you think about it, perspective is everything. We humans tend to make a big deal out of our tiny corner of the universe. We lose sleep over texts that say "K" instead of

"OK," or get pissed off when someone cuts us off in traffic. While out there in the cosmic Wild West, galaxies are swirling around each other like they're in a massive ballroom dance.

So yeah, the universe is big. And if you ever feel insignificant, just remember: you are! But so is everyone else. We're all just cosmic dust on this big galactic merry-go-round, so maybe it's okay to chill out about the little stuff. After all, when the universe is this mind-bogglingly huge, your parking ticket really doesn't seem that important, does it? And that guy who cut you off in traffic—he must be in a hurry—slow down and let him.

"Stop trying to control the people around you. When you 'let them' be who they are, you gain control over your own emotional peace."

Mel Robbins

Now, let's zoom back in a bit and bring it closer to home. Out of those 2 trillion galaxies, we'll focus on just our cozy corner: the Milky Way. Inside this galaxy, we've got hundreds of billions of stars. Our sun is *just one* of those many stars, and our little planet Earth? One of eight planets orbiting it.

Do you have your calculator out yet? Because this math is mind-blowing!

Zooming in even more—on Earth—there are about 8.5 billion people (as of this writing—and the human population is growing exponentially). Think about that for a second. You are one of 8.5 billion humans, each living unique lives with different cultures, languages and experiences.

Yet here you are.

You're <u>one person</u>, reading <u>these words</u>, on this tiny planet, orbiting one star in a galaxy full of stars, surrounded by trillions of galaxies. The fact that you're here, at this moment, reading this book, is nothing short of miraculous. The odds? Astronomical.

That's the power of perspective. On the one hand, you might feel insignificantly small in the grand scheme of things—and in some ways, you are. But on the other hand, the fact that you exist, with the ability to think, reflect and wonder about your place in this enormous universe, is extraordinary in its own right. From this perspective, our smallness becomes a kind of magic: it highlights how precious and unique our experiences truly are.

So the next time you're feeling overwhelmed by life's little annoyances—whether it's a never-ending to-do list or trying to find your keys for the millionth time—just remember: zoom out. Like, *way out*. Because when you realize you're a tiny human on a tiny planet in a galaxy filled with billions of stars, suddenly, that email you forgot to send doesn't seem so world-shattering. It's a humbling, mind-blowing perspective shift that can make the big stuff feel small and the small stuff feel, well, almost non-existent.

Turning Obstacles into Opportunities

Your life will be one big series of challenges. The challenges don't stop—they just keep evolving. One after the other. Some challenges are small and others big. It'd be pretty ridiculous if we didn't figure out how to handle these challenges along the way.

> *"I am not what happened to me,*
>
> *I am what I choose to become"*
>
> *Carl Jung*

Some challenges are massive, like the ones world leaders face while trying to keep the peace or solve global crises. And then there are the other challenges—like realizing you're one egg short of your pancake recipe and having to awkwardly knock on your neighbour's door in your slippers and robe. Hoping—*praying*—they don't judge you. So, yeah, life's full of hurdles, but they come in all sizes—some are world-shaking, others are just world-changing...for your breakfast.

Many of the struggles we face in life are deeply tied to our perception of them. When we encounter obstacles, our default response is often to view them as barriers, things that stand in our way and prevent us from moving forward. But what if we could reframe our perspective and begin to see those very challenges as opportunities?

In *The Obstacle Is the Way*, Ryan Holiday discusses how the Stoics believed obstacles present hidden opportunities, serving as the way forward rather than setbacks. Holiday is a modern expert in Stoicism and refers to the words of Marcus Aurelius, *"The impediment to action advances action. What stands in the way becomes the way."* This concept encourages us to view challenges not just as roadblocks but as opportunities for growth and personal resilience. It highlights the importance of *eliminating inefficiencies* on a daily basis.

For example, if you're faced with a job loss, this setback—while initially painful (and stressful)—can transform into a valuable opportunity. It provides you more space to reassess your path, seek and develop skills that align with your passions or explore roles that feel more fulfilling and meaningful. As Holiday suggests, reframing hardship in this way doesn't ignore its difficulty but recognizes that overcoming it can propel us toward new strengths we would have never known were possible.

"When one door closes another door opens, but we often look so long and so regretfully upon the closed door that we don't see the ones open for us."

Alexander Graham Bell

I repeat—<u>life is a never-ending list of challenges</u>. It's up to you how you handle them. Resilience seems like a skill worth mastering. Reframing challenges into opportunities for growth can serve us well in the long run.

I'll take it one step further. Seeking out difficult challenges is healthy for you and it's where the real growth happens. Do hard things and don't be afraid to fail. Failure can serve as the best teacher you've ever had (with the right perspective).

"Don't fear failure. Not failure, but low aim, is the crime. In great attempts, it is glorious even to fail."

Bruce Lee

When Bruce Lee talks about failure, you listen. After all, this is a guy who made getting kicked in the face look like an art form. It's in moments of discomfort and uncertainty that we often experience the greatest growth—exactly the kinds of moments where Bruce would be calmly delivering a roundhouse kick to the situation and reminding you to *be like water.*

When you're stuck in a tough spot or sweating through challenges, that's where the magic happens. Bruce knew that mastery wasn't achieved in the comfort zone. The comfort zone is the enemy of progress. Sure, we'd all love to sit around in a mental recliner, sipping on lemonade, waiting for success to come and tap us on the shoulder. But as Bruce would tell you, that's not how greatness is built.

Those who see challenges as stepping stones toward mastery are the ones who are most likely to succeed. They thrive on the challenge. They show courage in their pursuits. They don't quit after the first stumble or when things get tough. Instead, like Bruce, they embrace discomfort—not as a sign of failure, but as an essential, even exciting part of the journey.

> *"Failure is a learning experience. You can either turn it into a tombstone or a stepping stone."*
>
> *John D. Rockefeller*

Growth doesn't happen when things are easy. It happens when you're out of breath, a little bruised and questioning whether you're even headed in the right direction. Growth happens in the wake of your failures. It's your opportunity to take a look at the situation and re-evaluate what went wrong. This is when the magic happens.

So, I challenge you to be resilient in your own life. Don't shy away from discomfort or difficulty. Lean into it. When you hit those rough patches, remember—they're not roadblocks; they're opportunities for real growth.

Bruce would tell you that failure isn't the end—it's a teacher, a sparring partner in the ring of life. If you see challenges as part of the process, they stop being obstacles and start becoming opportunities. So, next time you're struggling, just ask yourself, "What would Bruce do?" He'd probably throw a punch, smile, and say, "This, too, is part of the journey."

The Attitude of Gratitude

Gratitude is like a secret superpower. Every challenge, obstacle or setback is met with a 'thank you.' It allows you to approach difficult situations from a positive mindset. Instead of saying "I have to" [insert task here], begin saying "I get to." Come to it from the perspective of gratitude.

"I have to" workout today sounds a lot different with a pinch of gratitude. Instead, saying "I get to" workout implies you are grateful for a healthy body that works, you are grateful for an opportunity to work on your health and you are giving your body the respect it deserves.

According to Shawn Achor's *The Happiness Advantage*, approaching situations from a place of gratitude can do more than just make you feel all warm and fuzzy—it can literally rewire your brain for happiness and success.

Think of it like this: your brain is constantly playing the world's longest highlight reel, but you are the one who gets to choose the clips. Focus on the failures, the frustrations and that one time you spilled coffee on yourself during an important meeting, and you'll start feeling like the universe is out to get you. But flip the script, and suddenly, you're seeing the small wins, the kind words and the simple joys—and the world starts looking a whole lot friendlier.

Achor points out that our brains are naturally wired for *negativity bias*—basically, we're way better at spotting the bad stuff than appreciating the good. It's like having a hyper-vigilant security system that goes off when you burn your toast but ignores the fact that you've got a loving family, a sunny day outside or the perfect playlist queued up.

The problem is when we focus on what's lacking or what's going wrong. We amplify those feelings of dissatisfaction, stress and fear—kind of like accidentally turning the volume all the way up on your least favourite song.

But when you practice gratitude, you're telling your brain to change the channel. You start looking for the good, the blessings and the small moments of beauty that often get drowned out by the noise of everyday stress. And the best part? Your brain listens. By shifting your focus to what's going well, you not only boost your mood but also your resilience. Your brain becomes anchored in what's *working*, not what's broken.

Achor also illustrates an important point about the relationship between happiness and success. Most people operate under the premise that success needs to come first in order to be happy. "I'll be happy when I…" But people have it all wrong. Learn to be happy first, and success becomes inevitable.

Gratitude also has residual benefits to those we love and sets off a ripple effect. Whenever you express your gratitude to the world, it positively affects another person. They can, in turn, pass this on to another, then another. Next thing you know, your entire social circle is an army of thankful people ready to take on the world!

"I alone cannot change the world, but I can cast a stone across the water to create many ripples."

Mother Teresa

So, next time you're feeling overwhelmed, take a moment to shift your perspective. Instead of replaying the day's disasters, ask yourself: what went right? Even if it's something small, like finding a decent parking spot or the fact that your Wi-Fi didn't crash during a crucial call. Gratitude can transform your experience.

Practicing gratitude doesn't mean ignoring pain or hardship; instead, it allows us to balance those experiences with the good that coexists alongside them. Research has shown that regular gratitude practice can improve mental health, increase resilience and even lead to a greater sense of life satisfaction.

Keeping a gratitude journal—where you write down a few things each day that you're thankful for—is a simple yet transformative habit that can shift your entire perspective on life. A few years ago, I started using the voice notes app on my phone. I recorded gratitude messages to myself. I also began leaving messages for my daughter to add to my legacy files (more on that later). I often go back and listen to them. Makes me smile every time.

More about gratitude prompts and practices in the downloadable PDF on our website.

Expanding the Timeline

I get it—when a crisis hits, it's all hands on deck! You experience a wave of emotion—a sense of urgency—and think, this is it, this is the end! Let's fix this now!

But the truth is we often get stuck in short-term thinking and short-term solutions. Like when we try to "solve" our problems with a knee-jerk reaction—kind of like slapping a Band-Aid on a leaky pipe and thinking, "That should hold."

In life, these quick fixes feel good at the moment, but much like that pipe, they usually end with us standing in ankle-deep water, wondering how it all went so wrong. When we're focused solely on the immediate discomfort of a situation, we tend to make decisions based on fear or desperation rather than wisdom or long-term strategy. When we get stressed, uncomfortable or hit with uncertainty, and suddenly, we're making decisions like we're in a real-life game of Whac-A-Mole—just trying to smash whatever problem pops up first.

But when we zoom out and *expand our timeline*, we start to see that many of the challenges we face today could lead to something better tomorrow. Maybe that job rejection is actually nudging you toward a career path that'll make you happier in the long run. Or that bad breakup is clearing the way for a healthier relationship—once you stop binge-watching rom-coms and eating ice cream straight from the tub, of course.

When we recognize that our life has an expiry date, we can navigate uncertainty with more grace (and fewer unnecessary freakouts). It's like switching from panic mode to *Bruce Lee mode*—calm, collected and ready to dodge whatever life throws your way with the smoothness of a martial arts master. Instead of scrambling to fix things immediately, we can ask ourselves, "How might this challenge actually help me grow?" It's a much cooler question to ask than, "Where's the duct tape?"

Sure, there will always be moments when short-term relief is tempting, like eating an entire pizza to deal with a bad day (not that I'm judging). But when we expand our perspective, we start to make decisions that aren't just about soothing our present discomfort but about building a future we actually want to live in.

Full disclosure: I'm a Green Bay Packers fan. (queue the boos) There is no way I'm writing this entire book and not throwing in a Vince Lombardi quote somewhere. He had more memorable quotes than your grandpa at Thanksgiving dinner, believe me. The one that really sticks out is simple: *"Who you are tomorrow begins with what you do today."* How true is that?

Expand the timeline and ask yourself, "When I'm on my deathbed looking back at my entire life, will I be proud of myself?" Do you really think you'll regret taking that risk on your career or asking out that pretty girl? Heck no! You will regret all the chances you didn't take.

After all, that career move made you millions and that pretty girl—she became your wife and the mother of your children. She's the best thing that's ever happened to you! Imagine your life without her! Now, this is the kind of wisdom that makes you feel ready to take on the world. Be proud of yourself when your time comes.

Lombardi knew that greatness wasn't built overnight—it was crafted one day, one decision at a time. If you need a little extra motivation, just imagine Vince Lombardi standing over you, yelling, "What's the delay?!" You'd get moving pretty fast, wouldn't you?

So next time you're about to make a fear-based choice or a knee-jerk reaction, take a breath, zoom out, and ask yourself: "Will this make sense six months from now, or will I look back and think, *'Well, that was my duct-tape-on-a-pipe moment'*?"

It's all about perspective.

Consider this for a moment: the difficulties you face today might be the very experiences that prepare you for a future opportunity. A heartbreak now could be what opens you up to deeper, more meaningful connections later. A career setback could redirect you towards a path that aligns more closely with your passions and values. This broader view reminds us that life is not a straight line but a journey of twists and turns, each playing a role in shaping who we become.

The Observer's Perspective

One powerful technique for shifting perspective is to step outside your own limited viewpoint and take a good, long look at yourself—like a fly on the wall, or better yet, like a judge on a reality TV show. It's basically like watching your life on Netflix, but instead of bringing the drama, you're calmly reviewing the chaos, sipping metaphorical tea, and thinking, *"Wow, that plot twist was unnecessary."*

When you become the observer through the lens of mortality, you create space between yourself and your reactions, which is so much better than getting swept away by every little emotion like you're starring in your own emotional soap opera.

This observer's perspective lets you view your thoughts and feelings as temporary—like clouds passing through the sky—rather than thinking, *"This is it. This anxiety I'm feeling is now my entire personality. I am Captain Panic."* Instead of getting consumed by the intensity of the moment, you can take a step back, stroke your imaginary beard, and think, *"Ah, yes, fear of the future again. Classic. Let's see how long this one sticks around."* Spoiler alert: It never sticks around as long as it seems.

This, too, shall pass.

So, the next time you feel overwhelmed by the intensity of the moment, try stepping into the role of the observer. Watch the emotional drama unfold like it's the season finale of a reality show—full of chaos but way more entertaining when you're not in the middle of it. Remember, it's always more fun to sit in the audience with your popcorn, calmly watching things spiral out of control, than to be the one running around on stage trying to fix everything with a broken microphone.

Be Like Water

In case it's not obvious, I'm a massive Bruce Lee fan. I mean, the guy could throw a punch so fast you'd need a slow-motion camera just to see it—plus, he makes kicking butt look effortless and cooler than anyone else ever could.

But what really gets me about Bruce is his uncanny ability to dive into the twists and turns of the human mind and then explain it in a way that actually makes sense. He wasn't just about epic movies; he was about mastering your mind, which is somehow even cooler than the flying kicks.

"Be like water making its way through cracks. Do not be assertive, but adjust to the object, and you shall find a way around or through it.

If nothing within you stays rigid, outward things will disclose themselves. Empty your mind, be formless."

Bruce Lee

Embracing a fluid identity means accepting that we're not stuck in one role or one version of ourselves forever. Embrace and celebrate the process of aging and evolving as a person. It's liberating! Life is constantly changing, and we're allowed to change with it.

Think of yourself as a river—sometimes you're calm and smooth, other times you're rushing and roaring, but you're always moving. When obstacles show up (because they will), you don't have to crash into them over and over again like a stubborn wave. Instead, like water, you find new paths, flowing around challenges, adapting as you go.

This mindset is especially freeing during times of uncertainty. When life throws you a curveball—a job loss, a breakup or the "really stupid" things you said at the company Christmas party—you don't have to cling to the idea that you've failed or that your worth is tied to that one role or label. It's not the end of your story; it's just the end of one chapter. Being fluid means seeing change not as a threat but as an invitation to rediscover who you are in this moment and who you're becoming next. It allows you to write a new chapter.

So, instead of panicking when things don't go as planned, ask yourself, *"What would water do?"* Would water get stuck trying to hold onto an old identity or outcome? No way. Water just keeps flowing, adjusting and moving forward. If a new path opens up, it flows right into it—no resistance, no fear of change.

"No man ever steps in the same river twice, for it's not the same river and he's not the same man."

Heraclitus

Remember you Must Die

Memento mori brings it all together: reframing challenges into opportunities, practicing gratitude, expanding our timelines, being that fly on the wall in your life and embracing that Bruce Lee-level fluid identity are all enhanced with the ability to see ourselves as temporary.

We can break free from the mental boxes we lock ourselves into. Life will always throw curveballs, but how we *choose* to view those curveballs can be the difference between hitting a home run down the left-field line or ducking under the bleachers in a panic (you baseball fans know what I mean).

When we realize that our perspective can be flexible, we suddenly gain the upper hand. We're no longer stuck in one way of thinking, like someone trying to fit a square peg into a round hole. We become more adaptable, resilient and—let's face it—much more pleasant to be around. Seriously, nobody wants to hang out with the person who's forever complaining about life's lemons. Be the person who makes lemonade, or better yet, starts a lemonade stand!

Sure, sometimes things might be falling apart, but instead of freaking out, we can calmly grab some popcorn and think, *"Ah, another plot twist. Let's see how this one unfolds."* Life's going to get chaotic, but with the right perspective, you'll not only survive it—you might just enjoy the ride.

"This is the true joy in life, the being used for a purpose recognized by yourself as a mighty one; the being a force of nature instead of a feverish, selfish little clod of ailments and grievances complaining that the world will not devote itself to making you happy."

"I am of the opinion that my life belongs to the whole community, and as long as I live it is my privilege to do for it whatever I can. I want to be thoroughly used up when I die, for the harder I work, the more I live. I rejoice in life for its own sake."

"Life is no 'brief candle' for me. It is a sort of splendid torch which I have got hold of for the moment, and I want to make it burn as brightly as possible before handing it on to future generations."

George Bernard Shaw

Chapter 4
It's a Numbers Game

I think it's fair to say that we all want to live a long, happy and healthy life. Filled with great friends and family. After all, you picked up *this* book about living with purpose in the face of mortality. Maybe you were eyeing the self-help shelf, thinking, "Hmmm. A little pep talk about purpose and maybe a side of 'living forever' wouldn't hurt."

Most of us would rather contemplate the meaning of life on our own time—like later—after watching the entire catalogue of Netflix, doom scrolling social media and definitely after our yearly existential crisis during tax season. But here you are, ready to face it head-on.

Picture your future self: decades of joyful experiences under your belt, too many family gatherings to count (you know, the kind where someone inevitably brings up politics) and a life so fulfilling that your retirement hobbies involve seeing the world, knocking down your golf handicap to single digits and perfecting your cocktail-making skills.

Imagine getting to watch your kids, your grandkids and maybe even great-grandkids grow up and become little versions of you—with all your best traits and, well, maybe a few of your quirks, too. And after all that living, you reach a grand old age, surrounded by the love of your family, peacefully drifting off in your own bed, having lived a life bursting with beautiful moments. Honestly, I hope you get every single one of these blessings. Because if anyone deserves a cinematic, heartwarming fade-out, it's you.

But let me be clear—this chapter is about the numbers—and the numbers are not always in our favour. The chances of you experiencing all of these joyous moments are not guaranteed; in fact, they're even unlikely.

This isn't meant to sour you or diminish your dreams. Instead, it's an invitation to embrace life's impermanence as *motivation*—to really live your life the way you want, with purpose and intention. Recognizing the limits of your time here isn't about loss; it's about fully appreciating the beauty of each fleeting moment and using that knowledge as fuel to live deliberately.

Time is your most valuable asset.

According to the World Health Organization, the global average life expectancy is around 71 years. I know—I'm doing the math in my head, too! Wait...carry the one...oh, hold up, that means I only have about 27 years left! Whoa—now that's a shift in perspective. Suddenly, the whole "live each day like it's your last" thing feels a lot more real.

Now, don't get your knickers in a knot just yet—Life expectancy is a complex measure shaped by many factors: Access to healthcare, quality of diet, economic stability, and even cultural practices. On top of that, this is a *global average*: Lots of people need to live longer than 71 for it to be an average! See, changed perspectives again.

In Canada, for instance, the average life expectancy is about 82 years, which is reflective of its well-developed healthcare system and stable food supply. Similarly, in the United States, the average lifespan is slightly lower, around 78 years, influenced by access to healthcare and varying lifestyle factors.

In many developing nations, however, the numbers reveal a starker reality. Due to limited healthcare, nutrition challenges, and economic factors, life expectancies in countries like Nigeria, Somalia and Chad average around 59-64 years. This lower average reflects the hurdles these populations face in basic healthcare access, quality food and water supplies and stable living conditions.

On the opposite end of the spectrum, countries like Japan and Switzerland enjoy some of the longest life expectancies, reaching approximately 84–85 years on average. This longevity is often attributed to balanced diets, active lifestyles, strong social support systems and comprehensive healthcare.

When we look at these numbers, they reveal something profound: life, whether it's 50 or 85 years, is essentially a *collection of finite moments*. You can't control where you were born or the conditions you grew up in. You can, however, fill these moments with meaning.

To help visualize this, imagine your life laid out on a giant grid of squares, each square representing a single week of your life. Now, let's assume you're one of the lucky ones who make it to the ripe old age of 90—that's a grid of 52 squares across and 90 squares down.

Each week, the squares get filled in one by one and slowly make their way across the grid. Each year that passes, we're on to the next row. And then the next. Another week passes, and another square is filled in. There's no going back to erase or change it. Each one is permanently inked, reminding us that life moves in one direction, and every single square is a moment—one week—waiting for us to fill it purposefully.

Your Life in Weeks

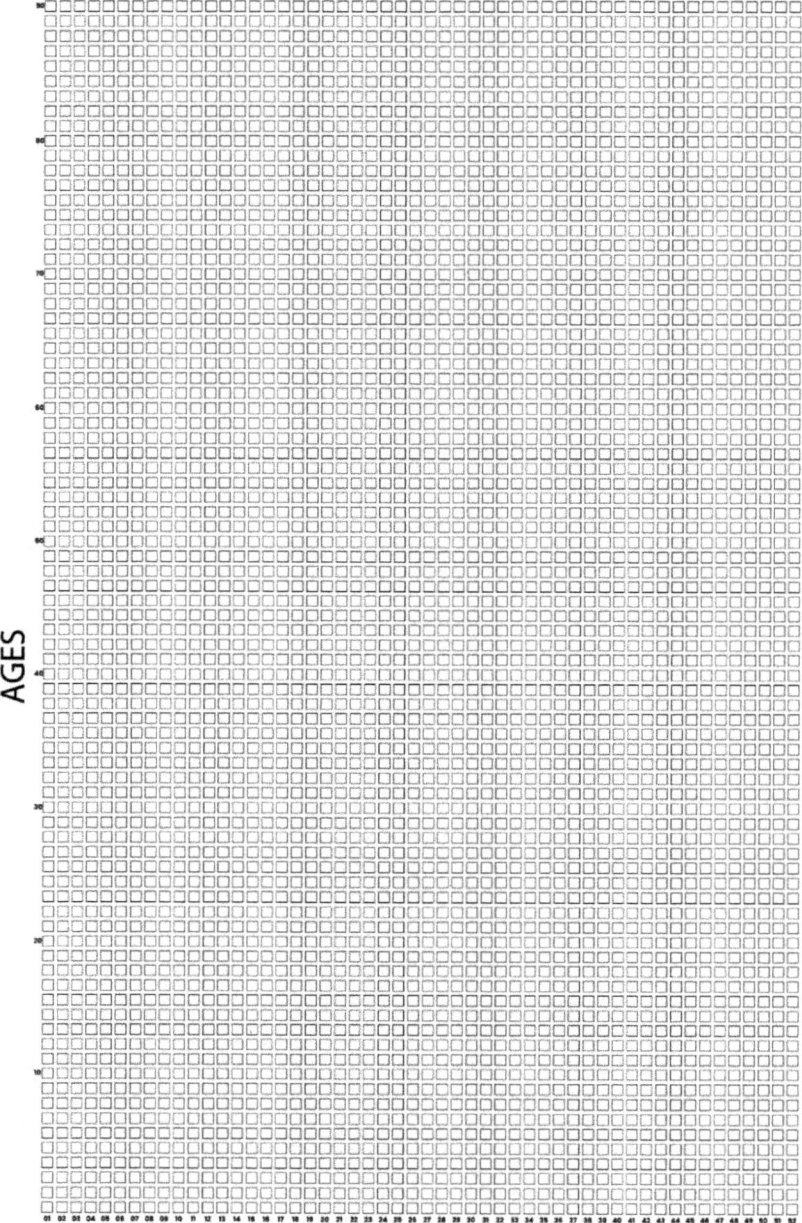

AGES

WEEKS

Where are you right now on this grid? This image is not here to intimidate or discourage you—after all, you're reading this book because you want to be real about your mortality. This image is meant to serve as a reminder that your time on earth is finite, but the moments are yours to shape. Each day, month or year to come is a blank slate, waiting for the memories we choose to create. In this one-way journey, the question becomes: how will you fill your squares before they're all gone?

The fleeting nature of life gives us an invitation to live it fully, making deliberate choices about how we spend our time, how we invest in relationships and how we pursue what truly matters to us. Go after those goals!

The main purpose of this chapter is not just to *see* numbers but to truly *feel* them and to recognize that the finite nature of life is the very thing that makes it meaningful. Maybe, just maybe, the beautiful part about this journey lies in its *impermanence*.

I invite you to slow down a bit. Just…take it all in. Breathe. Look around at all the beauty surrounding you. Admire the houseplants you've somehow kept alive against all odds. Bask in the glory of your kids and their many accomplishments. Yes, the same kids who have been known to start epic sibling battles over things like who gets the blue cup or who touched whose elbow. But, hey, in between those moments, they're also pretty amazing.

Take pride in their school projects, even if half of them look like something straight out of an abstract art museum. Cherish their sports games, where you'll cheer your heart out, no matter how many times they run the wrong way down the field. The projects and the sports are here for a short time.

Soon, the house will be quiet again—the chaos dies away. You'll be an 'empty nester' wondering what to do with your time. The time you get to spend with your kids doesn't last forever. Cherish it.

Life's beautiful moments don't always come with fireworks. Sometimes, they show up as the warm glow of a kid's smile or that rare but glorious moment when all the laundry is actually folded. Take it all in—because, in this one-way ride, those moments are the real wins.

Focus Question: What do you remember about last weekend?

Seriously—stop reading for a second and think about it. What did you do?

Time has a funny way of slipping away when we're caught up in the rhythm of our lives. Maybe you spent it with friends, enjoying those spontaneous moments of laughter and connection, or maybe you were ticking off a list of errands, crossing off one thing after another.

Think about it. What did you do? Who did you spend it with? What memories did you create? When you're not paying attention, the days seem to blend together, and before you know it, the weekend is over. Back to work! But how much of it do you actually remember?

We often rush through our days, blindly thinking about the next thing on our to-do list, checking off tasks, or just trying to get to the next moment. It's easy to get lost in the flow of time without fully engaging with the present.

Maybe there were conversations, sights or feelings that slipped under the radar because you were focused on something else. Maybe there was a great opportunity to help someone in need that passed you by. When was the last time you paused to appreciate the little things—like a warm cup of coffee in the morning or a random moment of joy that made you smile?

I'm not here to endorse a lazy lifestyle. You can only sip so many 'perfect coffees' before life demands you get up and do something. Part of your legacy is what you were able to accomplish. It's the impact you leave behind and the ways you invest your time, talents and energy. That's not something you get from hanging out in a hammock all day. But how often do we miss meaningful moments because we're too wrapped up in our to-do lists or worrying about what's next?

The irony about time is that it moves faster when we don't consciously reflect on it. Our brain is great at filtering out details when it's in "autopilot" mode. The less we think about time, the faster it slips away.

It's like the universe's inside joke—"Oh, you weren't paying attention? Too bad, that was *last year!*" Our brains are practically masters of editing out the boring parts, gliding through our daily routines on autopilot so smoothly that entire weeks can disappear.

Ever get home from work and suddenly wonder, "Wait, did I even drive home?" I know I have. That's autopilot in action. It's handy for survival (no one wants to analyse every step of brushing their teeth), but it's also why you look up one day and realize that somehow the 2000s were over two decades ago and then you wonder why kids nowadays don't know every word in the intro song to 'Friends.' (I can totally see you 40-

somethings singing every word and 'quick clapping' your way through the song—You know who you are)

When I was a kid, my grandfather caught me rushing around his workshop, probably getting ready to "help" him on a project I had no business touching. He was an old-school kind of guy, took his time with everything—measured every cut three times, sanded every corner until it was smooth enough to shine, and could spend an hour just organizing his tools.

Painful to watch as a youngster—believe me! He watched me buzzing around, and then he said, *"Hey, slow down, Michael. Take your time with things; that's how you make 'em last."*

Time is just zooming by while we're busy juggling a thousand tiny fires. You're answering endless emails, trying to figure out what's for dinner (again), shuttling kids to soccer, dance, karate and piano—basically training them for a marathon in scheduling.

Meanwhile, you're desperately "liking" everything on your social media feed so your cousin doesn't message you, "Hey, did you see my post?" The irony is the more you're scrambling to check items off your list, the faster time seems to run laps around you. You blink, and that dentist appointment you scheduled six months ago is already here (and somehow, *still* inconvenient).

You're constantly caught off guard, thinking, "Wait, it's Friday *again*?" Time slips away while we're in the trenches worrying about things like why your houseplant is looking at you funny, wondering why you didn't find the time to water it. Before you know it, you're Googling "When did Blockbuster close?" and realizing that it was probably around the time you still had time to stop and notice things (and to "be kind, please rewind").

The lesson here? Snap out of 'autopilot' now and then—take a conscious look around, savour a moment or two, and maybe, just maybe, we can slow time down a little. Or at least be awake for the ride!

It's one of the great paradoxes of life—how quickly time seems to pass when we're in the middle of it, but how slowly it often feels when we reflect. We are so immersed in the present moment, living day-to-day, that we don't fully grasp how much time has passed until we take a step back and look at the bigger picture.

—--------------------------------

Let's explore a few scenarios that illustrate how time can slip away without us even realizing it:

Six weeks later, You visit your niece or nephew and, without thinking, exclaim, "How did you get so big?" A toddler's growth is visible in the way their clothes no longer fit, the way they talk and run and the milestones that come and go. It's almost like you can measure time in the form of their changing size and abilities.

But the funny thing is, *the same 6 weeks have flown by for you, too*—only it's less visible on the surface. The changes in your life, while just as significant, aren't always as easy to pinpoint. In fact, when you reflect on those six weeks, you may realize that you hardly even noticed how fast the time passed. The moments spent in the rat race of daily routines, meetings or random tasks just blur together.

Six months can feel like it flies by in an instant—you catch up with an old friend over lunch and suddenly realize, "Wait, has it really been half a year?" It seemed like just a few weeks ago, you were chatting, but now, after you swap stories, it hits you: a lot can actually change in a short span. Jobs evolve, new hobbies emerge and unexpected challenges pop up. Time, in the daily grind, can feel sluggish, but looking back, it moves fast.

One Year Later: Anniversaries and holidays remind us of another year gone by, and we often find ourselves asking if we've really gotten closer to the goals we've set.

Dan Sullivan's book *"The Gap and the Gain"* is a great reminder to stop, look back and "measure backwards" to see just how far you've come in that one-year blink. Instead of lamenting that you're not yet a world-renowned chef or CEO, it's about recognizing, "Hey, a year ago, I didn't even know how to chop an onion, and now I can make pasta from scratch." Focusing on these incremental gains brings positivity and motivation.

Ten years might as well be a lifetime—new jobs, new homes, maybe even new family members. Nearly every part of your life might be different, from the habits you have, where you live or the people you spend time with. After all, nearly every cell in your body has regenerated in a decade; if you feel like a new person, well, you kind of are!

In 100 Years, everything familiar will likely be unrecognizable. The home you worked so hard to build will have cycled through many owners, probably renovated a dozen times over until it looks like a sci-fi movie set. The possessions you valued—the shoes you 'had' to have, the phone you couldn't live without—will either be relics in a museum or collecting dust in a junk shop. That handbag you once guarded with your life? It might be either long lost or the "vintage" item some teenager picks up as a cool retro find or an accessory to their Halloween costume.

As for us? In 100 years, our lives, habits and quirks will be only faint memories. Kept alive only in old photos or stories *if we're lucky*. The stories that do linger will be told by your elderly great-grandchild—and they might only be broad sketches, leaving the finer details to fade as time keeps marching forward.

After all, in the grand scope of things, our personal imprints are more like tiny footprints in the sand, washed away as the tides of time surge forward. Still, there's something almost comforting in knowing we're part of a bigger, ongoing cycle— just as the people before us were. So, if you want to leave a mark, make it a good one—or at least one that might make the future smile!

When we look at the numbers like this, time has a funny way of slipping through our fingers, doesn't it?

Think back to that 52x90 grid, each square a week of your life. *Go look at it again.* How many squares have you filled already? Are they full of color, or are they grey and bland? And more importantly—how many do you have left?

Let's break it down.

If you're 20: First of all, good on ya for picking up a book about mortality. I know I wasn't in the frame of mind to think about it in my twenties. You're probably looking at that grid and thinking, "Oh, I've got *plenty* of time. Practically all my squares are blank!" But be honest with yourself—How many of those squares are already filled in with Netflix marathons, social media scroll-a-thons and existential crises that end in midnight snack runs? Now's the time to decide which squares you're going to fill with things you'll actually remember—or better yet, things that matter to you.

A small piece of advice: Spend time with people who bring you up a level and make you think deeply about life and your place in the world. Recognize that your time on this earth is not guaranteed and the world is full of distractions for you; focus on what brings you joy.

If you're 40: Okay, the grid's starting to fill up, huh? Somewhere along the way, your squares started vanishing faster than your metabolism. You're filling them up with career milestones, mortgage payments and a lot of drives to and from the hockey rink, soccer field and dance studio.

But let's get real: how many of those squares have you spent just keeping up with the pace of life without stopping to think about what you want to look back on? It's not too late to grab some squares for yourself, you know.

If you're 60: By now, the grid's looking pretty colourful with life events. Some squares are proudly packed with memories; others might be a blur of daily routines, grocery lists and "Did I turn off the stove?" moments. But you've still got some squares left.

Which ones are you going to fill with that "someday" you've been talking about for years? Maybe it's time to cash in on those retirement plans and fill a few squares with pure adventure—or at least fewer meetings.

If you're 80, You're probably looking at that grid and marveling at how many squares you've actually filled. Some are filled with love, laughter, even heartbreak and maybe even a few embarrassing moments you'll never share. It is a mosaic of colorful experiences!

But you've still got some left! This means right here and now is the perfect moment to reflect, to savor and to fill those last squares with whatever brings you joy—whether it's time with family, naps in the sun, or finally mastering that hobby you never had time for.

No matter where you are on that grid, it's all about how you spend what's left. Time is a one-way street, but every square that lies ahead is a chance to make a choice. A choice to live with purpose and—most importantly—to slow down and notice the ride.

So, the question is, what will you do with your remaining squares?

"When I'm thinking about my death, I can see very clearly who I wanna be. I can see how I'm spending my time. I can see if I'm pleased with what it is that I'm doing. And if I'm not, well, my death is asking me to change it all the time."

Mel Robbins

We seem to be careful with our material things like money, possessions and careers—tracking our spending and budgeting with the vigilance of a hawk. Seemingly always needing more to achieve happiness. Yet when it comes to time—our most precious resource—we tend to give it away like it's an endless free sample.

Time, unfortunately, doesn't play by the same rules as other resources. We can't "see" the hours we're spending, which makes it all too easy to misplace them on mindless scrolling, checking off our endless to-do lists or waiting for an "extra" hour that will never really appear.

Imagine time as an hourglass that only flows in one direction, with each grain of sand representing a moment slipping away. If life were a "pay as you go" plan, those grains would be the hidden fees we never think about until we notice the balance dwindling. Each week, day or even hour that flies by is one less piece of your finite lifetime, and no "customer service agent" can grant you a refund.

When you start seeing time this way, every interaction with loved ones, every little success and even every moment of joy takes on a new weight. Not only are these moments meaningful, but they're tiny investments in the life we're building.

So next time you're tempted to bail on that coffee date with a friend or push off a step toward your dream project, think of it like passing up a rare, priceless gem—because that's what these moments really are.

Time may be invisible, but it's constantly offering us golden little windows to connect, create and grow. Sure, it's easier to believe there are plenty of "somedays" in the future, but each one of those tiny chances you let slip is a little bit of your life that you won't get back—and there are no guarantees about your future days either.

"The 'good old days' are right now."

Tom Clancy

All those coffees, dreams and steps forward are the ingredients that make life not just long but full. The memories and relationships we create are the real currency, the stuff that builds a life worth remembering.

So grab that latte, take that next step—even if it's a little nerve-wracking or a little risky—because that's where life is actually happening. And who knows? You might just look back one day and thank yourself for not choosing the couch and Netflix...every time.

Memento Vivere

Remember, you must live.

Memento Mori is our wake-up call. That jolt that makes us take action in our lives. That swift kick in the rear that we all need from time to time. Hey pal! Stop wasting your time. You're going to die someday!

Memento Vivere, on the other hand, is our reminder to live fully and to use the time you have left wisely and with intention. In order to do this, we need to cut out the things that no longer serve our highest goals and double down on the things that bring us joy and excitement.

So, in this theme, we'll focus on the things that will bring value to your life: cutting out the crap that doesn't serve you, building meaningful relationships with those you love, saying yes to adventure, making memories and mastering your time.

Mortality has a funny way of reminding us that time is precious. But instead of letting that be a downer, let's use it as motivation to dive deeper into who we are and who we want to become. Let's look at this theme as a life audit of sorts. For us to objectively look at where we are in our lives, who we spend our time with, what we worry about and why we're not living up to our fullest potential.

But hey, if you're thinking, "I've already got all that figured out." Then flip right to theme 3. All good.

Chapter 5
Trim the Fat

So, here we are—Chapter 5, *Trim the Fat.* And no, we're not switching to a wellness blog or signing you up for a 5-day juice cleanse. This isn't about transforming you into some relentlessly glowing health guru or stripping away every last guilty pleasure. We're simply going to objectively look at your current life and cut loose the dead weight that's been dragging you down like an overstuffed suitcase.

We've all got that stack of dead weight. You know what I'm talking about. It's the bad habits, the negative people, the gossip we engage in, the infinite scrolls, the gaming, the screen time and the late-night snacking that leaves you feeling exhausted and more cynical than an unpaid intern.

We're not talking grand gestures of self-renewal here. You don't have to flee to the Himalayas or live in a Wi-Fi-free yurt in the middle of nowhere (although if that sounds appealing, go for it!). No, this chapter is about cutting loose what doesn't *serve you* so you can reserve your precious energy for, well, living with purpose!

Think of this chapter as your chance to do a life cleanup— taking a good look at everything you've gathered over the years—stuff, habits, worries—and asking, "Does this still serve me? Is this actually making me happy? Does this serve my higher purpose?" I challenge you to have the courage, to be honest about your answers and have the fortitude to be selective with your time and attention. Do you have the willingness (there's that word again) to make meaningful changes in your life?

We need to be selective about what we pay attention to and what we choose to care about. Harvard psychologist William James explains *selective attention* like this:

"Millions of items of outward order are present in my senses which never properly enter my experience. Why? Because they have no interest for me. My experience *is what I agree to attend to."*

This idea hands you the power—and yes, maybe even the *responsibility*—to decide who and what gets a VIP pass into your life and who's left standing behind the velvet rope. It's your call to choose what's worth your attention and what's simply background noise. You have that choice. Make it wisely.

Imagine it like curating your own personal guest list: Emails? You'll be seated way in the back. Gossip? Sorry, no time for you. Endless social media scrolling? You're not even on the list. Friends who lift you up? Front and center! The beauty is that you get to decide who makes it into your inner circle and what gets put in the "thanks but no thanks" pile.

Think back to our 52x90 grid. Each little square is a week of your life, a moment waiting to be filled. By choosing intentionally, you're shaping your experience, deciding which squares go to people and passions that lift you up, and letting the less important things fade into the background.

It's like you're painting a mural with your grid. Each square represents a brushstroke—*a choice*—a moment where you've directed your attention and energy. Will it be splashes of time spent with loved ones, squares filled with creativity, new adventures or those tiny joys that make life richer? You hold the brush—every square is a chance to create something meaningful, something that reflects what truly matters to you.

So choose wisely, and make that grid a masterpiece. Embrace this opportunity to polish your existence down to the essential bits and do so with the knowledge that *none of us get out alive.* We may as well enjoy the ride with a lighter load and a fuller heart.

So here's what we're doing: we're loosening our grip on the things that bog us down and just don't make the cut. And the best part? No guilt. Imagine the epitaph: "Here lies someone who decided to enjoy life more by ignoring that email and leaving that toxic group chat." And really, what better legacy could there be?

The People Problem

Let's talk about your "friends." Yes, those lovely folks who fill your social calendar but might actually be sneaking into your life with the charm of a coffee spill on a white shirt. You know the ones I mean: the gossip-spreaders, the chronic complainers, the friends who think a conversation with you is just a warm-up to interrupt you every five seconds. The friends that are living in a constant state of comparison, unhappy in their own lives and incapable of expressing joy for you. They're the ones constantly measuring their lives against yours, making you wonder if you accidentally wandered into a one-sided competition.

And, of course, let's not forget the experts in the art of the never-ending pity party. They're not just airing a grievance now and then; they've practically built a little nest in their misery, invited you over for dinner, and are generously serving up a heaping portion of "everything is terrible."

So grab some popcorn because, with these friends, every hangout is a front-row seat to the drama. But here's the question—do you *really* want to keep filling your precious squares with their eternal gloom-fest?

"You become the average of the five people you spend the most time with."

Jim Rohn

If you're constantly surrounded by negativity, bad habits or people who are more committed to complaining than to improving, it starts to rub off on you. Imagine going to a paint store every day—you're bound to come home splattered with something. The question is, are you coming home with inspiration or just smudged with their leftover grievances?

If your "friends" seem more focused on pulling you down than lifting you up, it might be time for a bit of pruning. It's like the 'crab in a bucket' mentality. Imagine a good number of crabs inside a big bucket. If one of the crabs decides to escape, what do you think the other crabs do? Yep - they team up and pull that crab right back in—making the escape almost impossible. Don't fall into this trap in your own life.

This doesn't mean you have to ghost anyone overnight or launch into a mass unfriending spree. But it does mean you need to set boundaries that protect your well-being. You're not obligated to be everyone's emotional support animal, especially if it's weighing you down and draining your own happiness.

Here's a reality check for your friends: Just like you, they also have the power to improve their own situations. They have the ability to decide what they allow into their own lives and make changes if they're willing. They can pick up this book too! So don't feel guilty! While you can lend an ear or a shoulder, the choice to grow, improve and lift themselves up is ultimately theirs. You're not responsible for fixing their problems, and sometimes, holding yourself accountable and setting clear boundaries can inspire them to take more responsibility for themselves. Heck! It may actually inspire them!

It's not selfish to choose friendships that are mutually supportive. You deserve to be around people who encourage you and add value to your life, not constantly weigh it down. So, start setting boundaries, let your friends know where you stand, be proud of yourself and allow them to make their own decisions about improving their lives—just as you're doing with yours.

I'll leave you with this metaphor: Friends are a lot like a tree. Some are the roots and the trunk of the tree—strong, steady and nourishing. They are with you for the long haul. Their roots run deep and create a strong foundation. They're the ones you can always rely on, supporting you through all seasons and storms.

Then there are friends that represent the branches: They're with you for most of life's journey, and they're growing with you, but every now and then, a storm rolls through, and some of them break off. These friends may be close for years, but sometimes life pulls you in different directions.

And then there are the leaves. They come into your life in a beautiful rush, filling your days with colour and excitement, but they're only there for a season. They drift away when the winds change, leaving behind memories that may fade over time.

Each friend, whether a trunk, branch or leaf, plays a part in the story of your life. Each with its own unique beauty.

Social Media: Where Problems Go to Fester

Social media can be a fantastic way to stay connected, get some laughs and maybe even learn a thing or two. But it can also be a deep, murky pool of negativity, misinformation and pointless outrage. Ever find yourself in a heated argument with someone's second cousin twice removed over something that barely affects your day-to-day? Suddenly, you're locked in a battle of words with a 'keyboard tough guy' you wouldn't recognize in real life, and for what? Is there an actual winner in these online arguments? What's the prize?

Then there's the curious phenomenon of our "friends" and followers. In our quest to accumulate them like trophies, we often forget that social media is a highlight reel, not a documentary. People only post the best parts of their lives— their vacations, their achievements and the perfect selfies that have been filtered to high heaven. Where's the photo of them fresh out of bed, hair askew, before they've brushed their teeth? Those candid, less-than-flattering moments rarely make the cut.

The truth is that this curated presentation of their life creates a skewed reality that can make everyone feel like they're falling short. It's easy to compare your day-to-day life to someone else's highlight reel and feel like you're losing the race. It's also unfair to expect your spouse, friends, siblings, parents and children to live up to these unrealistic expectations.

The reality is *you become what you consume.* That includes what you see, read, listen to and who you interact with online. If you're constantly taking in content designed to rattle you or make you feel inadequate, it's bound to take a toll on your mental state. It's like junk food for the mind: an occasional indulgence won't hurt, but binging on outrage and clickbait day after day will only make you feel more anxious, frustrated and drained.

So, take a step back and really look at your feed. Consider doing some "social media spring cleaning." Start by unfollowing accounts that leave you feeling bad about yourself or spread negativity. Stop posting stuff that you know can be harmful to others. Do you really need to keep up with every acquaintance you've ever had? Especially if their posts just add clutter to your mind? Get rid of them too. If they're meant to be in your life, they'll find their way back.

If you choose to be on social media, curate your feed to bring you joy, teach you something new or simply make you feel like the best version of yourself. When it comes to social media, quality beats quantity every time. Instead of focusing on how many "friends" you have, focus on the quality of those connections. You deserve to surround yourself with authenticity, not an endless stream of polished highlights.

Food for Thought

Let's get one thing straight—I'm not here to lecture you into a raw-vegan-no-sugar-no-gluten-no-fun lifestyle. That's not what this book is about. If that were the case, I'd be the world's worst motivational speaker, and you'd probably find me locked in a pantry, crying over a bowl of kale.

This book is here to help you appreciate—and actually make the most of—the time you've got on this planet. And let's be real, it'd be a whole lot easier if you're cruising through life in a body that's actually, you know, fueled with real nutrition.

Think of your body like a car you have for life—you'll NEVER get to trade it in. If that were the case, would you remember to change your oil every 3 months, change the wiper blades and put on new tires once they're worn out? Of course, you would! Because if you don't, eventually, you'll be stuck on the side of the road looking for a tow truck.

Now, I can hear some of you saying, "If we're all going to die anyway, why bother?" But here's the thing: as you inch closer to the bottom of that grid, your health starts feeling a lot like currency. When you're young, you might feel like the world's immortal snack enthusiast. But one day, you'll find yourself eyeing the stairs and thinking, "Is it worth it?" So, think of taking care of yourself now as an investment. You're putting a little "healthy interest" in the bank so that in the future, you can enjoy the ride without needing to negotiate peace treaties with your knees.

> *"Taking care of your body is a form of respect you owe to yourself."*
>
> *Chris Williamson*

But seriously, if you're regularly eating (or drinking) stuff that makes you feel like you've just swallowed a rock, it might be time to rethink a few choices. I mean, do you really want to feel like a sloth that just ran a marathon?

Now, I get it: life is busy. Not everyone has time to prepare quinoa bowls every Sunday while practicing yoga. But being a little more mindful about what you eat can seriously improve how you feel—like, "I actually want to get off the couch and do something" kind of better.

If most of your meals come straight out of a bag or box, maybe it's time for a little culinary adventure. Try swapping a few of those bagged snacks for something fresh and balanced. You don't have to turn into a gourmet chef overnight; just make it a point to toss a couple of fruits and veggies into the mix.

> *"Let food be thy medicine and medicine be thy food."*
>
> *Hippocrates*

I mean, it's easy to imagine Hippocrates with a wooden spoon in one hand and a bottle of kale juice in the other, passionately preaching about the benefits of whole foods.

But really, it's true! This is a book about accepting our mortality and living with purpose! Taking care of your body is part of the deal! When you fuel your body with nourishing food, you're not just giving it energy; you're also supporting your brain, which is basically the command center for everything you do—like getting through that endless Zoom meeting or keeping your sanity while dealing with a work deadline.

So, embrace the idea that food can be a mood booster. No need to go full-on health guru; just sprinkle in some intention. Who knows? You might just find that a little more colour on your plate leads to a bit more colour in your life.

It's Not Your Job to Rescue Everyone

Trimming the excess in your life doesn't mean it's your job to rescue everyone who's not quite on your level. We all have that one friend—the human tornado—who seems to attract drama and chaos and is perpetually in "crisis mode." You know the one: their life is like a soap opera that never gets cancelled.

While it's great to be supportive, you're not a superhero in spandex, and it's definitely not your responsibility to carry everyone else's weight—unless, of course, you're training for the Olympic team in emotional weightlifting.

Sometimes, stepping back and letting people sort through their own stuff is the most respectful thing you can do—for them and for yourself. If you're constantly bailing out the sinking ship of your friend's chaos, you might just end up in the water with them, flailing around and wondering how you got there in the first place. You didn't sign up for the "Life Raft of Drama" tour! It gives them the space to grow and learn while freeing them up to focus on the people and things that genuinely add value to their lives—like that friend who always makes you laugh or that hobby that sparks joy.

The purpose of this book is simple yet powerful: *your time is your most valuable asset*, and you need to protect it like a mother bear guarding her cubs. So, trim the fat and let go of that self-imposed duty to "save" everyone. You're not running a charity for emotionally needy friends—this isn't a reality TV show where everyone gets a free ride on your emotional rollercoaster. Your time and energy are finite, and they deserve to be spent on things that truly enrich your life.

Invest your precious hours where they'll make the biggest difference for you. Maybe that means diving headfirst into binge-watching a new show that makes you laugh so hard you snort or tackling that backyard project that's been giving you the side-eye for far too long.

Ultimately, this book is your guide to reclaiming your time and focusing on what genuinely matters. Life is too short to be caught up in the chaos of others; it's time to prioritize your own happiness, health and sanity. So take a deep breath, let go of the emotional baggage, and remember: Your time is too valuable to waste on drama that's not yours to carry.

Here's the paradox that often happens—get ready for it—*The more you focus on yourself, the more space you create for others.* Amazing, isn't it? It's like tidying up a cluttered room; once you clear out the junk, you not only feel lighter, but you also find space for the things (and people) that truly bring you joy.

You're not just saying goodbye to negativity; you're making room for the friendships that matter, the passions that ignite your spirit and the opportunities that enrich your life. Embrace this journey of self-focus, and watch how it transforms not only your world but also the way you relate to others.

You'll find yourself attracting more genuine relationships because you'll be a *magnet for positivity*, not a lifeboat for emotional shipwrecks. So, dive in and invest in the experiences and relationships that truly light you up—you'll be amazed at the positive ripple effect it creates!

Chapter 6
Relationships

"We humans are social beings. We come into the world as the result of others' actions. We survive here in dependence on others. Whether we like it or not, there is hardly a moment of our lives when we do not benefit from others' activities. For this reason, it is hardly surprising that most of our happiness arises in the context of our relationships with others."

The Dalai Lama

Contemplating—*and truly accepting*—our mortality is like standing completely naked before the vastness of existence. It peels back every illusion, every distraction and every comforting lie we tell ourselves to avoid the raw truth about our lives: *we are temporary.* The paradox lies in how it manages to be both utterly terrifying and profoundly liberating all at once.

This acceptance is a heavy burden to bear. It brings with it a weight that lays heavily on your shoulders. Yet, in that moment of clarity, there's a strange feeling of inner peace. A beautiful sigh of relief overcomes you and the weight begins to lift.

The senseless trivialities that once consumed you—status, money, power, possessions and grudges—all just fall away, revealing the quiet truths you've always known but never dared to face. The result: you are truly thankful to be alive and you are thankful for the people in your life.

Accepting our mortality doesn't just strip us bare; it lays us wide open, exposing the core of who we are and what we hold dear. It forces us to confront the questions that truly matter about our relationships with others: Who do we love, and how deeply? What connections define our lives? How will we be remembered when our time here ends? Mortality challenges us to move beyond mere existence and embrace the fullness of truly living—to cherish, to connect, to dance in the rain and to love fiercely while we still have the chance.

Picture this scene for a moment: It's the final chapter of your life, and you're in a bed in the hospital, surrounded by the people who matter most to you—family and friends—the ones who've shared your laughter, your tears and your soul. You feel it in your heart; you know the end is near. Your eyes move slowly across the room, locking with each face that has been a part of your journey. Their tears stream freely, but you meet them with a quiet, steady smile—a smile that says, *It's okay. I'm ready.*

One by one, you summon the strength to tell them what's in your heart. "I love you. I'm proud of you." The words aren't just spoken—they're etched into their hearts, meant to stay with them long after you're gone.

Your breath grows shallower now, and the rhythm of your chest is slowing down. Their faces change; panic, heartbreak and love swirl together as they grip your hand tighter like it's the only thing anchoring them to the world. "We love you," they whisper, voices breaking, "Thank you."

You take one final breath, deep and deliberate, and let it go. Softly, gently, it drifts into silence. The room is still now, but it's filled with a profound, aching love. The circle of life has reached its conclusion—not with fear, but with peace, connection and the unshakable legacy of a life well lived.

This is a profound scene. Raw emotion.

These were the final moments for Fred C. Ryall. My father-in-law passed away on October 6, 2023.

We were all together with him. Telling him we loved him. As he took his final breath, a tear rolled down his face.

It was the most profound moment I've ever experienced.

Who will be there for you in your final moments?

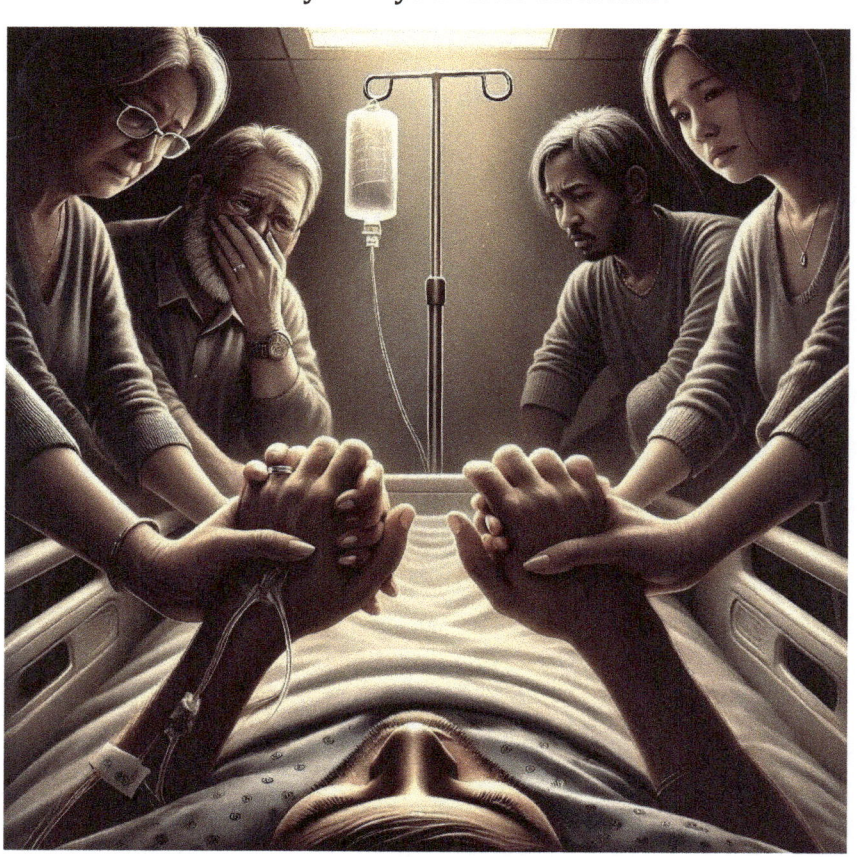

What makes this scene magical is the *relationships and connections* with all the people in that room. They are the ones who will carry your memory forward. They are the ones that will tell crazy stories about you. They are the ones who will comfort the younger generation as they mourn your loss. Despite life's distractions, they were the ones who always mattered most.

At some point in your life, you will likely find yourself in a moment just like this. Saying goodbye to a loved one. Maybe you've already been there, and the memory is etched into your heart. I have been there, witnessing the last breath of my father-in-law—it was the most profound and humbling experience I've ever had. He died peacefully, surrounded by his family. It instantly put everything into perspective. I am so thankful to have known him, and being there for his last breath was a gift. I whispered to him before he was gone, "I will always take care of your daughter. I love you." He just looked at me—he no longer had the strength to speak—he gave me a slight smile and a small tear streamed down his face. I knew it meant a lot to him.

When you're craving the ultimate reality check, bring yourself back to this scene. Imagine you're the one lying in that bed, the steady rhythm of the heart monitors gradually slowing. Surrounding you are familiar faces; their eyes filled with tears, their hearts breaking in real-time. Now ask yourself—who will be there? Who will be the ones holding your hand, refusing to let go? What regrets, if any, will still weigh heavily on your heart?

Every day is another opportunity to shape that future. Master the art of building relationships that matter—deep, honest and meaningful connections that stand the test of time. Because when that moment comes, it's not your achievements, possessions or status that will surround you. It will be the people whose lives you touched, whose hearts you loved.

So, live right now, fully and intentionally. Build a life that makes the 'future you' proud. A life where, in your final moments, you can look around the room, see the faces you cherish, and know you truly lived and you're truly loved.

Be ready for that scene. You've been rehearsing for it your entire life.

"Embrace the breadth of friendships that comes with youth and prioritize the depth of friendships that should come with age."

Sahil Bloom

Let's hit the pause button for a second. Take a deep breath— or two, maybe three if you need it. Seriously, go ahead, breathe it out.

This is some heavy stuff.

We need to take a moment to clarify one of the main goals of this book: For you to become that energetic and awesome elderly person everyone admires—the one who's out walking every day with friends, not because you have to, but because you genuinely enjoy it.

The one who can host family gatherings and whip up a mean pasta dinner so good that people fight for seconds, even if they're on a low-carb diet. You've got a vibrant social life, always the first to RSVP and somehow the last to leave, effortlessly blending wisdom with a killer sense of humor.

I mean, seriously, who wouldn't love being that person? You're the grandparent who still crushes it at trivia night, the friend who remembers everyone's birthday and the neighbor who always knows the juiciest gossip—*but in a kind, endearing way, of course.*

> *"Treat your body like a house you have to live in for another seventy years. If something has a minor issue, repair it. Minor issues become major issues over time. This applies equally to love, friendships, health, and home."*
>
> *Sahil Bloom*

So, let's aim for that future version of you: healthy, vibrant, happy and surrounded by people they love and admire. You are living proof that age is just a number when you've got pasta and good vibes on your side.

The key to it all is meaningful relationships.

In a landmark study conducted by Harvard University, spanning over 75 years, Dr. Robert Waldinger and a team of researchers uncovered a profound truth: good relationships are key to a happier, healthier life. This study, one of the longest-running of its kind, followed hundreds of people across generations, carefully documenting everything from physical health markers to emotional well-being. The results were as clear as day.

"Good relationships keep us happier and healthier. Period."

Dr. Robert Waldinger

It isn't the number of relationships that matters; it's the quality and depth of those relationships. Much like a tree draws its strength from the depth and resilience of its roots, not the number of its branches. The most meaningful connections are those that anchor us, the ones that nourish our growth and provide stability through life's storms.

"Loneliness kills…It's as powerful as smoking or alcoholism."

Isolation, according to Waldinger, takes a significant toll on both mental and physical health. While strong, meaningful connections foster resilience, improved happiness and even longer life spans. This isn't just about staving off loneliness, though; it's about investing in genuine, supportive connections that carry us through life's challenges.

This revelation screams what we all secretly know: humans need deep connection. And guess what? Contemplating and accepting your own mortality has a funny way of helping us cut through the noise and focus on the relationships that actually matter.

When we accept that the people in our lives won't always be there—and neither will we—we begin to cherish moments more deeply. A conversation with a loved one becomes more than just a routine exchange. A hug with your best friend lingers longer. We say yes more often to meaningful experiences—and we say no to things that don't serve our higher purpose. The time we spend with friends and family transforms into an irreplaceable treasure.

So don't hold back. Dive in and make those connections that light you up. Call that friend you've been "meaning to text" for six months and actually catch up. Forgive your parents. Seriously, forgive your parents—they are human too. Say yes to the things that excite you—or terrify you in a good way. Plan that epic vacation, whether it's a dreamy getaway to Italy or a glamping trip in a yurt. You do you.

Spend your money on things that genuinely matter to you. That fancy coffee maker? Totally worth it if it makes you happy every morning. That concert with your favorite band? Go for it!

Let go of that grudge—it's not like they're paying you rent to live in your head anyway. The only person whose grudge is hurting is you—and you deserve better.

Laugh too hard, take too many pictures and don't be afraid to look a little silly along the way. These are the moments that stick, the stories you'll tell over and over again, the memories that will make you smile decades from now when you're the one teaching others how to truly live.

Have the conversations that matter, even the awkward ones where your words come out all wrong but somehow bring you closer in the end. Because the last thing you want is to find yourself in that heartbreaking moment—watching someone take their final breath—realizing there are things you never said. Now, that is a pain that cuts deep.

Perhaps it was an argument with your best friend, unresolved, leaving you to wonder what might have been if only you'd reached out. Life is too fleeting for "should haves" and "if onlys." Speak your heart now—while there's still time to be heard.

On a personal note—I recently had a deep and meaningful conversation with a good friend of mine after his dad passed away. His dad had been his rock—always there with steady advice, an easy laugh and one of the kindest men you'd ever meet. I always had wonderful conversations with him. But in the final years, his dad developed a form of dementia, slowly fading in and out of recognition. Watching his father's memories slip away was devastating for him, his mother and his two brothers, an erosion of someone who had once been so vibrant and so sharp.

As we sat together beside a campfire, he shared something that struck me deeply. *"You know what bothers me the most, Mike?* A tear was streaming down his face. *I don't remember the last thing we talked about. I'm racking my brain, but I can't seem to remember. It breaks my heart."*

Although his dad passed only a few months earlier, it had been *years* since they had a meaningful exchange. He shook his head, clearly wrestling with the fact that those last conversations— the things he had assumed he'd remember forever—were now foggy and slipping out of reach.

I could feel the weight of it—the ache of realizing that, for all the years they had shared, there wasn't a clear, memorable parting moment. A tear was streaming down my face now. It was extremely emotional.

Instead, there were only fragments of conversations, little snapshots from the final days and pieces of a man who had once been whole but was now wrapped in the murkiness of disease. His dad's condition had made those last months unpredictable; conversations blurred, moods changed without warning and he often had to just hold on to whatever fleeting connection they could find in a given moment.

But as we talked, I reminded him of something I had once heard: *maybe it's not the final words that matter, but the sum of all the words spoken and shared throughout their years together.* Maybe it's not the last conversation that defines a relationship, but the years of conversations that fill the gaps in memory, the ones that shape who we are.

Developing a healthy relationship with our mortality has a way of bringing into focus what truly matters. When we come to terms with the finite nature of life, the value of each relationship becomes strikingly clear. We start to understand, deeply and inescapably, that life is too short for connections that only scratch the surface. This realization urges us to invest our energy in relationships that nurture us, ones that fill us with a sense of meaning, warmth and genuine companionship.

After this conversation with my friend, I couldn't stop thinking about my own father and the relationship we had built over the years. There was a sudden—*almost urgent*—need to know him on a deeper level to understand the experiences, values and dreams that had shaped him. I realised that, like any meaningful relationship, this one deserved my full attention— an openness to learn more about who he was beyond the father I'd always known.

So, I decided to ask him a few questions—ones that would open up the possibility for deeper conversations and insights. I made it clear that he didn't need to answer them right away and that he could take all the time he needed. I wanted to give him the space to reflect and respond when he was ready so each answer would carry his fullest thoughts and memories.

When I shared the idea with him, he gave me a look of amused surprise, grinning as he joked that I was "way deeper than he'd ever expected." But I could tell he was touched—excited, even—by the chance to share his story and his thoughts in a way he hadn't done before. It was like he had been waiting for the invitation, and now that it was here, he seemed elated to dive into the memories, philosophies and lessons he'd collected over a lifetime.

I encourage you to connect with someone you admire in your life. Someone you've always looked up to. Ask them about their lives, their dreams and their experiences. Trust me—they will be more than excited to share what they have learned along the way.

This process didn't just help me understand him better; it deepened the connection we shared. It brought new dimensions to a relationship that had already shaped me profoundly, reminding me that even the people we think we know best have parts of themselves waiting to be discovered. And in knowing him more fully, I found myself more grateful than ever for the father, mentor and friend he had become in my life.

Here were my questions:

1. *What were some of the greatest experiences in your life?*

2. *What experiences would you still like to have before you die?*

3. *What "little things" do you enjoy most in life today?*

4. *What do you realize now that you took for granted when you were younger?*

5. *What things did you love doing as a kid that you never talked about?*

6. *What big goals or dreams did you have when you were young?*

7. *What advice would you give me now that you haven't been able to tell me yet?*

8. *What are your biggest regrets in life?*

9. *If you could go back in time and change just ONE thing in your life, what would it be?*

10. *If you could put a sign on a billboard to tell the world ONE message - what would it be? And why?*

Mortality teaches us that being *truly present* with our loved ones is one of the greatest gifts we can offer—and receive. It invites us to put down our phones, stop worrying about tomorrow and simply be there for each other, fully engaged.

When we understand that our time is limited, the moments we share become more precious. The everyday laughter, shared stories, comforting silences and even the difficult conversations take on a deeper significance.

This awareness can also soften our hearts, urging us to approach others with greater kindness, empathy and patience. We learn that there's no room for holding grudges or letting small misunderstandings fester. Instead, we start to focus on showing up with love and understanding, creating a legacy of compassion that endures. By being kind and present, we let our loved ones know that they are truly valued, creating memories that will sustain them long after we're gone.

In the end, accepting our mortality opens our eyes and our hearts. It isn't about filling life with things; it's about filling it with people who matter. And it's in these meaningful, loving relationships that we leave behind something enduring: a piece of ourselves woven into the lives of those we cherish.

This legacy of love and presence becomes our true gift—a lasting reminder that our lives were rich, not in time, but in connection.

Practices for Nurturing Relationships

Nurturing deep, meaningful relationships requires intentional effort. It's easy to get caught up in the distractions of daily life, but with a few simple practices, we can deepen our connections and create a lasting bond with those we care about. Here are a few strategies to consider:

Regular Check-ins

In a busy world, we often lose touch with the people who matter most. Scheduling regular check-ins—whether it's a phone call, a coffee date or even a quick text message—ensures that the relationship remains strong. These moments of connection don't have to be grand or time-consuming. The act of reaching out, asking how someone is doing and showing genuine care can mean the world to them.

Expressing Gratitude

Develop an attitude of gratitude. We often take our closest relationships for granted. Expressing gratitude is a simple way to let people know they are valued. Whether it's through a handwritten note, a text message or a verbal acknowledgment, small acts of gratitude go a long way.

The people in our lives should know the impact they've had on us. Reflecting on death reminds us that every interaction could be the last, which encourages us to express thanks more frequently.

Be Present

In our fast-paced, tech-driven world, we often engage with others while being mentally elsewhere. Being present and fully attentive to the person in front of you is a gift. Put the phone away. Seriously—put it away! Those memes and emails can wait! Human beings got on just fine for thousands of years without Instagram! Make eye contact. Listen deeply. Engage fully in conversation. Ask meaningful questions. Mortality has a way of emphasizing the importance of being fully present for others.

Practice Empathy

Empathy allows us to see the world through someone else's eyes. When we practice empathy, we deepen our relationships by showing others that we care about their feelings and experiences. Your legacy is about how you make people *feel*. Helping them feel seen and heard is a wonderful gift.

Mortality also helps us realize that everyone is fighting their own battles, making empathy an essential ingredient for connection. Think of the times when someone listened to you without judgment. Those moments likely left a lasting impact. Offering the same to others fosters deeper bonds.

Invest your Time

Relationships, like anything worthwhile, require time. This doesn't mean you have to spend every waking moment with someone, but it does mean prioritizing quality time. Whether it's a weekend getaway with friends, a family dinner or a simple walk with your partner, investing time in meaningful connections strengthens the relationship.

Schedule a monthly (non-negotiable) dinner date with your spouse, spend one-on-one time with your child and call your parents more often. When we view time through the lens of mortality, we see it as one of our most valuable resources, one that should be spent with the people we cherish.

Final Thoughts

Mortality might seem like a heavy topic, but let's be real—it's also a reminder to live in a way that makes your funeral *the event of the year.* Who's going to tell the hilarious stories about the time you tried karaoke after two margaritas or that one road trip where you got everyone lost but ended up finding the best taco stand? If you've nurtured your relationships, you'll have a lineup of people ready to roast you—in a loving way, of course.

Do you really want your eulogy delivered by someone who barely knew you, awkwardly muttering, "Uh... they were... nice?" Of course not! You want your best friend up there, cracking everyone up with the story of that time you devoured an entire pizza solo and proudly declared it was "for science." Or your sibling, gleefully sharing the greatest hits album they secretly recorded of your "shower show tunes performances."

That's the legacy you want—one full of laughter, love and all the ridiculous moments that made you—*you.*

By letting go of grudges and actually showing up for the people who matter, you're not just building connections—you're curating a legacy of laughter, love and memories so good they'll become legends. Life is too short for shallow relationships or unresolved drama. Go all in now, so one day, your friends and family are arguing over who gets to tell *the best* story about you at the buffet table.

Chapter 7
Making Memories

One of my favorite traditions growing up was the glorious mess-making that came after unwrapping presents on Christmas morning. My sisters and I had a very clear mission: create the *biggest* pile of shredded, crumpled, chaotic wrapping paper possible!

Every year, Mom would ask—no, beg—that we keep things "tidy" with the use of a garbage bag, a plea we ignored with joyful consistency. This wasn't just about refusing to clean up; this was about art. We aimed to create a wrapping paper mountain worthy of our Christmas morning efforts.

The look on Mom's face as she surveyed the scene of absolute paper carnage was priceless—she'd sigh, roll her eyes, give us that knowing smile and mutter something like, "Would it *kill* you to use a garbage bag?" We know she secretly enjoyed the show.

But by that point, we were already halfway buried in paper scraps, with just our faces peeking out like deranged gift-giving moles. To us, it wasn't Christmas morning until we had to literally dig our way out of all the paper and bows.

Dad, though? He looked at the mess differently. The bigger the mountain of torn-up wrapping paper, the more he grinned. He'd watch us with a huge smile, laughing at our efforts to bury ourselves completely in the aftermath of Christmas morning. He started wrapping our gifts in five layers of paper just to add to the mountain. He knew that the mess was just part of the magic, something that made the day feel more alive.

Sure, we had to dedicate the rest of our morning to cleaning up the carnage, but that was just part of the Christmas rhythm. After all, what's the point of Christmas if not a little chaos?

Nowadays, with my own family, Christmas is still nothing short of magical. The snow falls softly outside, blanketing the yard in the quiet glow of early morning. Inside, however, it's another story—our daughter wakes us up at 6 a.m.—on the dot—her little feet thundering down the hallway with more excitement than Santa himself. Weary-eyed but grinning, my wife and I stumble into the living room, clutching mugs of extra-strong coffee and we get ready for the big event.

As soon as the first present is opened, chaos ensues. Our daughter dives in, laughing as she turns the room into a mountain of shredded wrapping paper and tangled ribbons. And here's the best part: I'm right in there with her, adding my own creative touch to the festive mess. The paper pile grows and grows, and it's me now—*not* my wife—leading the charge to make sure that the floor is completely buried in wrapping paper by the end.

Every so often, my wife shakes her head, laughing as she tries to bring some order to the scene. I quietly grin when I see the parallels from my childhood.

"Can we *please* use a garbage bag?" she says, like a hopeful referee in a one-sided game. But our daughter and I just give each other a knowing look, the kind that says, "Yeah, that's not happening." We share a laugh at the exasperated looks we get, and, for a moment, I'm that kid again, grinning through a mess that feels a little bit like magic.

These days, my Christmas wish list is pretty simple—it consists of one item—a photo book from the past year. That's it. My wife puts so much thought and love into these books, pouring over photos and carefully arranging each page to capture every special moment just right. She knows how much

I cherish them, and every year, she outdoes herself, filling each page with memories that bring 'the year that was' back to life.

When she hands me that book on Christmas morning, we settle in, flipping slowly through each page. I can feel my eyes start to water as I take in the photos—our laughter, the chaos and the quiet moments and that one-of-a-kind love that makes our family ours. It's these memories, frozen in time, that make our Christmas and every day so wonderfully unforgettable. And so, one photo book at a time, my collection grows, capturing years of joy, one tear-filled page at a time.

It might sound almost too simple, but with each year that passes, I realize more and more that life is about collecting stories. That photo book, filled with random smiles, snapshots from road trips and blurry but cute images of spontaneous family moments, is worth more to me than any other gift. It brings the stories back to life again.

Think about it: When was the last time you looked back fondly on a random item you bought years ago? Probably never. Now, think about the last time you laughed over an old memory with family or friends. There's no contest. This is why we fill our lives with experiences, say yes to adventure and capture the little moments that turn into our favorite stories. And really, what better way to live than to look back on a life full of laughter, love and memories made with the people we cherish most?

I decided that I needed some perspective to help me write this chapter. What do other people think about this? So, I recently turned to a group of people with the benefit of retrospect— an average age of 83—to get their take on life, love and living with purpose. These are people who've seen it all, so I figured, why not hit them with the big question? One that is unbiased and promotes thoughtful responses: *What makes a meaningful life?*

I expected some philosophical deep dive, maybe even some regret for all the stuff they didn't buy. But overwhelmingly, the answer was this: *time spent with the ones you love and making memories.* Not one person mentioned the importance of owning the latest gadget or a fancier car. Nobody even mentioned a single material item.

No, they talked about memories—of family, friends, trips, laughter and the little adventures that made them feel alive. All of them would crack a smile when they were reminiscing about the amazing life they've had. Some even broke out into laughter when telling me a funny story about their past.

Most of them added the importance of loving your life partner and keeping the spark alive within their relationships. The older you get, the more time you'll be spending with the special person. Choose wisely. The lesson: don't undervalue the importance of selecting the right partner for you in life.

The most important decision of your life is who you choose to share it with. Life, my friend, is about gathering memories like you're some kind of joyful hoarder. Stockpiling snapshots of laughter, adventure and even those awkward family dinners. These are the things that matter. It's like a secret bank account full of priceless experiences you can tap into whenever you need a reminder of what makes life meaningful. So, say yes more often. Try new things, take way too many pictures and, most importantly, prioritize memories over material items whenever you can.

Be a Storyteller

The stories you tell become part of your legacy. They're not just fleeting moments; they're the threads that weave through the fabric of your family and friends' lives, shaping how they remember you. Over time, you become the bridge between generations, sharing the wisdom, humor and lessons of the past while leaving a foundation for the future.

"After nourishment, shelter, and companionship, stories are the thing we need most in the world."

Philip Pullman

So be the one who makes people laugh until they cry, who remembers the random details, who can say, "Hey, remember that time we..." and instantly bring everyone back to the moment. Being the storyteller of your own life is a gift you give yourself and everyone around you.

Years from now, when you're at the bottom of that grid, you won't remember the sleekness of your phone case or the brand of your coffee maker. But you *will* remember the time you got hopelessly lost in Italy, took a wrong turn, and found a tiny, family-owned pizza place that had the best slice of your life. Or the family camping trip where your kids ended up in the lake looking more like muddy, giggling otters than children.

One of my closest friends is a perfect example. He's notorious for exaggerating every detail to the point where we all just shake our heads, grinning. We look at each other and smile— *here he goes again.* The truth is, I admire it. It's what makes him special. I once joked that his gravestone should read, *"Never let the truth get in the way of a good story."* Comical but true!

He's already building a legacy through the stories he tells—and let's be honest, they're better for the embellishments! There's something timeless in those moments when we're all gathered around, sharing stories with laughter and maybe even a tear or two.

At the end of the day, it's these memories that carry weight far beyond any material thing. So be the storyteller of your own life, knowing that the best stories—the ones you'll tell for years and the ones others will pass on about you—are still waiting to be written, even if they go through a little 'broken telephone' modifications.

Say Yes More Often

One way to stock up on these moments is to get a little more adventurous with your "yes." Picture yourself standing at a fork in the road: on the left, comfort, and on the right, the unknown. Take the unknown path a little more often.

Now, before you panic, I don't mean you need to start skydiving or sign up for an underground fight club. No, it's simpler than that! It could be as easy as saying yes to a last-minute dinner invite or impulsively deciding to hop on a plane to a country where you know maybe three words in the local language (and where "yes" could get you a fiery bowl of soup you absolutely weren't ready for).

"The only impossible journey is the one you never begin."

Tony Robbins

There's a thrilling, borderline hilarious freedom that comes with saying yes. Remember that time you said yes to karaoke? In the moment, you might have wished the floor would swallow you whole, but now it's legendary! Your friends won't ever let you forget your pitchy but passionate rendition of "Livin' on a Prayer."

It's these ridiculous moments that make life richer, and that same epic karaoke night might just become the yardstick against which all future embarrassing moments are measured. Saying yes doesn't mean uprooting your entire life; it's about opening the door to a few more spontaneous moments, a little more adventure and a lot more laughter.

In the end, you'll find that the slightly embarrassing, often absurd memories are the ones that truly stick with you. Years down the line, those are the stories that become family classics, proof that sometimes, taking the road less travelled makes for a much better story. So go ahead, say yes, and see where it leads—hopefully, somewhere you can laugh about later!

See the World, Take Pictures

Travel whenever you can, and make sure you take plenty of pictures. Now, hold up—I don't mean snapping a shot of every meal like you're building a food blog empire. Sure, get a few classic scenic shots, but make sure to capture the real, imperfect moments that don't make it onto postcards: your kids grinning with gelato smeared all over their faces, that accidental thumb-in-the-frame covering half of the Eiffel Tower and let's not forget that time your whole family decided matching Hawaiian shirts would be "fun." These are the pictures that won't just remind you of where you went; they'll bring you back to how it felt to be there, with all the laughs, mishaps and joy that made the trip truly memorable.

When it comes to travel, it doesn't have to be exotic or come with a five-figure price tag. A weekend camping trip an hour away can be as epic as any international flight, especially when you consider the horror-comedy of assembling a tent at midnight while wrestling mosquitoes that seem like they came straight out of Jurassic Park. It's not the backdrop that makes the trip unforgettable; it's people you're with and the shared experience of getting lost, trying new things and laughing when things inevitably go wrong.

Because that's the magic of travel—you get to step out of your comfort zone and open yourself up to all the weird, wonderful, sometimes stomach-churning experiences this world has to offer.

Maybe you'll try sushi for the first time at a hole-in-the-wall joint and accidentally mistake the wasabi for avocado (a rookie error that you'll feel for days). Or perhaps you'll find yourself dancing with locals in a village square, badly out of sync but loving every minute of it. These are the things that add layers to your life—moments you can't buy or replace with any material object.

So pack your bags, keep your camera ready, and say yes to the trips, big or small. Years from now, it won't be the souvenirs that make you smile; it'll be the stories, the road trips, the photos and the beautiful, silly memories that only happen when you step out of the ordinary and into the unknown.

Embrace the Inside Jokes

As you fill your life with these memories, you'll notice an interesting (and very underrated) side effect: a growing stash of inside jokes with the people closest to you. These are pure gold—the kind of jokes that make no sense to *anyone* outside your circle and tend to surface at the most hilariously inappropriate times, like in the middle of a serious meeting or right before the wedding vows. Maybe it's a bizarre mishap from a road trip gone wrong or a totally random phrase that became your go-to code for *literally everything.*

Inside jokes are basically tiny time machines that transport you right back to the original moment. And the best part? The older you get, the more valuable they become. The mere mention of "Kevin's spaghetti incident" will still make you laugh until you're practically in tears—even if no one else knows why "spaghetti" makes you lose it. These are the stories that remind you of how it felt to be right there, caught up in the absurdity of the moment, fully alive and just barely holding it together.

So go ahead, take a minute and think about an inside joke with your bestie. Are you smiling now? Maybe even chuckling a bit? It's okay; no one's judging you. These are the jokes that have such power over you that just remembering them can have you snickering in line at the grocery store or suppressing giggles at a wedding ceremony.

Now is a good time to put down this book and call your bestie. Bring up your version of "The Spaghetti Incident!"

(And check in on them while you're at it :)

Let's be honest, though. If someone overheard your inside jokes, they'd probably think you've lost your marbles. But that's the beauty of it—they don't need explaining. They're just there, like little nuggets of absurdity that instantly take you back to those ridiculous, irreplaceable moments that no one else could (or would want to) fully understand.

When we break life down to its essentials, it becomes clear that the stories we tell—and the stories others tell about us—form a major part of our legacy. These narratives, filled with laughter, wisdom and love, are what carry us beyond the years we walk the earth. So, embrace the idea of making memories with the people you love and say yes more often!

Chapter 8
Mastering Your Time and Energy

Play Cribbage.

A friend of mine told me a great story recently about cribbage. His father, now in his late 70s, asked him one day if he ever learned how to play cribbage. My friend had no clue how to play cribbage and had little interest in learning. Being a busy guy, living in the city, and the fact the drive to his father's house was just under an hour each way, it was tough to make it all work. He was hesitant to commit at first, but his father insisted. He was confident that he could teach him the game very quickly.

So, every Sunday, they had a scheduled cribbage match. Week by week, my buddy began to understand the game and actually became quite good in short order. Still unable to beat his father, he grew impatient. He always could beat his dad growing up. He was a competitive guy.

A few months go by and he still hasn't won a single game. His father, with a playful smile on his face, insisted it takes time to learn cribbage and he'll be successful soon. As he gets better at the game, it requires less of his focus. He starts to focus more on the conversations with his father while they play cribbage. He begins to ask some thought-provoking questions and gained some insight into his father's upbringing and his family. He began to cherish the deep connection his father and his mother shared and he begins to understand his own views of the world. Every Sunday with his father turned into a great conversation (and some heated debates.)

But he still couldn't beat him at cribbage! It was beginning to bother him. One day, his father messes it all up and he fumbles the deal. My buddy realizes, at that moment, that his father has been cheating the whole time! He had developed a sleight of hand that went unnoticed for all the Sunday afternoons over the past few months! You're cheating? Seriously? Why do you invite me here every Sunday just to cheat at cards?

His father just sat there watching his son get upset. He says nothing. Just listening to the rant. "Seriously, dad, it's an hour each way to get here." His mom is listening to the mayhem unfold from the other room.

"Hey mom," he yells to the other room, "You know dad has been cheating the entire time at cribbage?"

There's a pause for a moment. Silence. His father is still silent, slightly amused. Then he hears his mom yell back from the other room, "I'm surprised it took you so long to figure it out! He's been doing that hand trick since we were dating."

His dad bursts into laughter! I mean uncontrollable laughter! His mom gets up from her chair and joins the boys playing cribbage. She takes one look at the father and she also bursts into laughter! They couldn't stop! For 5 whole minutes, the slight look at each other just evoked another burst of laughter.

As each minute passes, my buddy gets more and more pissed off!

His mom finally catches her breath to say something. My buddy is getting more furious by the minute. His father is barely catching his breath. "It was never about the cards, hunny." She is still laughing between each sentence, "Your father just wanted an excuse to spend time with you."

A look of stun on the face of my buddy. "You knew he was cheating the whole time?"

"Of course I did," she replies, "open your eyes next time."

His father interjects, "Want me to teach you backgammon next week?" His father still can't stop laughing.

"Now go wash up for dinner, you two!" Mom escapes to the kitchen. He and his father just stared at each other. However, this time, they're both smiling.

The moral of the story: say yes to cribbage.

An update on their cribbage game: They still play cribbage every Sunday. Except now, he's finally managed to win a few games.

———————————————

We live in a fast-paced world. It's easy to get caught up in the hustle and bustle that life brings. Constant distractions, notifications every 30 seconds on your phone, deadline after deadline at work and a Google calendar so colourful it looks like an abstract painting. Time just flies by, and we don't even get a chance to catch our breath.

A good friend of mine and I have birthdays 3 days apart. We've known each other since we were 6 years old. I remember him saying on our 24th birthday, *"Drake, six years ago, we were 18; six years from now, we'll be 30!"* I jokingly scoffed at him and dismissed it. But it stuck with me! Now I look back and realise that my 24th birthday party was 20 years ago! And my 30th birthday arrived a lot sooner than I expected.

When we reflect on these moments, they hit like a ton of bricks because they remind us of just how fast time moves. And the truth is, time *does* fly, whether you're paying attention or not. The earth keeps spinning around, the moon goes through its phases, and you take another trip around the sun. It's our choice—we can either let it slip away or use it wisely.

In this chapter, we'll dive into how thinking about our own mortality can help us appreciate time for what it really is: *our most valuable asset.* We will learn how to consciously slow down and be more deliberate with our time. We will learn how to live in the present moment and not let it go to waste. Your daily decisions matter—a lot.

"*Everything is cause and effect. If you don't move, nothing will move with you, and nothing will move toward you.*"

Michael J. Fox

Remember in *Back to the Future* when Marty realizes that even small decisions drastically change the future? (Or am I the only Marty McFly fan?) The same applies to your life. The choices you make today—whether you spend your Tuesday afternoon working on something meaningful that helps shape your ideal future or just crushing another bag of Doritos while binge-watching old TV shows—you are shaping your future, whether you realize it or not.

The truth is we can't hop in our DeLorean and gun it to 88 mph to rewrite the past. Time doesn't work that way—at least not yet. All we have is this moment, right here, right now. So strap in because this could be the wake-up call you need to stop letting life run you over and start living like you're destined for the future you deserve.

"Every morning, we are born again. What we do today is what matters most."

Buddha

Take a few moments and look back at the 52x90 grid from Chapter 4. Reflect on it again. Each week, you fill another square. One by one, they get filled in. Whether it's filled with new adventure and purpose or it flies by in a blur, it gets filled in anyway. Time is linear—a one-way street. You've got one shot to make it count. You can't keep putting off the things that matter in the hope that you'll "get to them someday." Life doesn't wait—and tomorrow is not guaranteed. It's the small things you do over and over that will truly add up over time. Those little daily actions? They're the building blocks of success.

Every tiny choice is a brick you're laying in the foundation of your life. Skipping that workout today might not seem like a big deal, but skip enough of them, and you'll see the cracks in your health. On the flip side, doing small, positive things consistently builds something monumental over time. This isn't about grand, sweeping gestures—it's about the power of consistency.

If you do just a bit of what matters every day, like saving $10 into a savings account, reading a few pages of a book, prioritizing your sleep schedule, writing a couple of paragraphs and checking in on close friends to see how they're doing, that effort will snowball. One day, you'll wake up and realize that those small actions have transformed into something big—whether it's a more secure financial future, a healthier body or even finishing that novel you've been dreaming about.

The Japanese call it *Kaizen*. This literally translates to "good change." The concept is simple: focus on small continuous improvement that comes from small incremental changes. Not massive changes all at once—small changes. Like laying your clothes out the night before to create efficiency in the morning or starting your day with a big glass of water instead of a sugar-filled breakfast. These small changes create momentum into something bigger.

Can you be 1% better than you were yesterday? A measly 1%? Now imagine doing that every day! You'd be 365% better after one year! This is why focusing on consistency, even if it feels minuscule at the moment, is crucial. It's like planting a seed into the soil—you won't see the tree right away.

In fact, you may not see anything for a while. But with daily care and a little bit of water, that small seed grows into something mighty. If you wait for the "perfect time" to plant the seed, you'll always be staring at an empty garden. Life doesn't give us the luxury of a pause button, and you can't hit rewind, either!

Your future won't be built in a day, but it is built one small action at a time. That's the true secret to mastering your time and energy—First, be honest about your habits and then start to focus on the things that matter to you and start doing them consistently; you're creating your best future one brick at a time. So start building now.

Understanding Time as Finite

Let's start with the obvious: *you're going to die*. But hey, so am I! And so are your neighbours, your friends, your siblings, the family dog and that weird-looking squirrel in the backyard. We're all in the same boat here! And while that may sound like a bit of a downer, it's actually the ultimate motivator. What *will* matter at the end of your journey are the things you can't put in a box: the impact you made on others, the relationships you nurtured and the lessons you passed down. These are your true legacy. These require you to be mindful of your time.

Most of us waste away our days on things that bring zero fulfillment. Becoming a victim of the trillion-dollar marketing industry, buying another "life-changing" gadget or an overpriced handbag, endless scrolling through social media, watching mind-numbing TV and attending *another* meeting that could have been an email. It's like running on a treadmill and expecting to get somewhere.

Try this exercise: Start to think about your time as a limited bank account—because when you do, you might start spending it more wisely. Imagine each day of your life represented by a balance in this bank account. The catch? You don't know how much was deposited when you were born, and no one gets to check the balance. Withdrawals happen daily, without fail. There are no deposits, no overdrafts and certainly no credit extensions.

So, how would you spend that unknown balance? Would you waste it on things that don't matter or invest it in moments and experiences that enrich your life? Every decision becomes critical when you realize tomorrow's deposit isn't guaranteed. Let's look at some practical steps to mastering your time:

Go to bed with a plan

Before you go to bed, take a moment to run the next day through your head. What are your goals for the day? Are you tackling them with confidence or with panic? What obligations do you have? When will I spend time on my fitness? Is it just a work day, or have you promised to finally fix that squeaky door or leaky faucet?

Who should you call tomorrow to see how they're doing? A loved one? A colleague? Spread your love and empathy to the people in your life that make it meaningful. Should you make an appointment with the dentist you've been ghosting for the past 18 months? Planning ahead isn't just responsible—it's your chance to dodge tomorrow's "Oh no, I totally forgot about that!" moments. And if you wait too long for that dentist appointment, you may be sorry.

We have the ability—and the technology—to set reminders for ourselves. All that is required is intention and a small dose of discipline. Go to bed with a plan for tomorrow. Make lists if you have to. Whatever works for you.

Master your Mornings

Most people spend their mornings like this—hit snooze a couple of times, check their phone, grab a shower, check their phone again, grab a bite to eat, check their phone again, drive into work—then they think, hmmm, what should I do today? By that time, it's 9:30 -10 am and they're playing catch-up for the rest of the day.

A powerful strategy, especially for early risers, is to *master your mornings.* This one can be a game-changer. My personal motto about this is to *"Wake up before the sun!"* Getting out of bed early is like hitting a secret button on the day. The rest of the house is snoring away and you're laser focused. Completing tasks, sending emails, reading books, meditating or going outside for a walk.

For years, I was a classic snooze-button enthusiast, but once I made mornings non-negotiable, everything shifted. I lead a very busy life and it can be hard to find the time. But do you know when I find time to write this book? Yep—*first thing in the morning!* I made it my mission to get up and spend 90 minutes on this book every morning before I went on with my day—no distractions.

There's something almost magical about those quiet early hours when the rest of the people in your world are still asleep. No deadlines and no distractions. It's just you and your thoughts—you have the freedom to focus on what truly matters to you.

"Early to bed, early to rise, makes a man healthy, wealthy, and wise."

Benjamin Franklin

By making your mornings non-negotiable, you take control of your day before the day takes control of you. It'll be hard at first. But as you stay consistent with it, it becomes easier. You'll be amazed at how much more you can accomplish, and the sense of peace and focus it brings will ripple through the rest of your life. Daily challenges will always be there, but you'll be able to tackle them with confidence and grace.

Control the Narrative in your Free Time

We all have *some* free time in our schedules. Whether it be the few hours before bed, the crisp Saturday morning, the extra hour in the morning you've created (because you've committed to mastering your mornings!), or your lunch hour throughout the week. These breaks in your routine are valuable. They are an opportunity for growth. It's your choice how you use these nuggets of opportunity.

"Your weekends can be used to escape the life you have, or they can be used to build the life you want."

Jari Roomer

I've heard it before: *'I can't wait for the weekend!'* or the ever-dreaded *'Is it Monday again?'* People barely get through their week, clocking in at jobs they hate, following the same rinse-and-repeat routine. Then the weekend comes, and instead of doing something meaningful, they blow their time and money on fleeting distractions—like buying another overpriced gadget, chicken wings and beer for Sunday football or working on that body imprint on their couch. And just like that, *bang*, Monday slaps them in the face again.

Free time is valuable. If your dream is to retire from work, escape the rat race, travel the world or accomplish something big, the weekend isn't just for your vices. It's your VIP pass to building that life you're dreaming about! It requires intention, and it's worth it every time.

Here's some harsh truth about life—nobody is coming to save you. Seriously. You're on your own here. Once I grasped that concept, my perspective changed completely. It's up to you to create the life you want. So stop treating your Saturday like a snooze button and spending your lunch hour 'like' every post you see on social media. Start treating your free time like a launchpad to the future and legacy you want!

Final Thoughts

At the end of the day, the clock started ticking on all of us the day we were born. But instead of being freaked out by that, let it be your greatest motivator. So ask yourself, what are you spending your time on? Are you investing it in things that bring you joy, growth and purpose? Are you utilizing the hours and minutes of your days on meaningful growth, or are you letting it slip away, one YouTube channel at a time?

Everyone gets the same 24 hours in each day.

This chapter isn't meant to make you paranoid about the clock. It's about helping you become intentional about how you spend your hours and manage your energy. After all, we don't get to choose how much time we have on this earth, but we are in control of how we use the time we're given. Make sure you're spending it on what really matters to you and to build the future you want. So when your time does come, and you're surrounded by your family on that bed, you can look back and think, "Yeah, I did it right—I'm proud of myself."

Chapter 9
Let it Go

Let it go, let it go

I am one with the wind and sky

Let it go, let it go

You'll never see me cry

Here I stand, and here I stay

Let the storm rage on

Elsa (Frozen)

You're not perfect.

But hey, neither am I. Neither is your neighbour, your boss, your cousin twice removed or your parents. We are human— *All of us*. There is so much power (and peace) in realizing that humans make mistakes, say things they don't mean, have a different perspective than you and maybe flat-out don't like you. So what? Figure out what drives you and stay true to yourself. You do you—and let that shit go!

In a world that constantly tells us to acquire more—more stuff, more money, more status—it can feel revolutionary to simply *let go*. But when we start thinking about death, as heavy as that might sound, it offers a unique clarity. Focus only on what you can control. Focus on how you operate on a daily basis and how you treat your time. Focus on how you treat people with empathy and gratitude and on how you see the world. Focus on shaping your perspectives and relationships. You're not responsible for how other people operate and feel. You're only responsible for you.

"We don't really heal anything; we simply let it go."

Carl Jung

This chapter is all about embracing the power of letting go not just of material possessions but of emotional baggage, longstanding grudges and the mental clutter that weighs you down. We all make mistakes. We have all done things we regret. Holding onto these things is like carrying a heavy backpack on the journey through life. When we strip away what's unnecessary, we lighten the backpack. And in doing so, we make space for what truly counts: meaningful relationships, unforgettable experiences and a life filled with meaning and purpose.

Let's take a page from the golf course for this one: *"Don't let your last shot affect your next shot."* In life, much like in golf, we have to let go of past mistakes, bad decisions and even successes. Just because you lost your ball in the trees—*again*—doesn't mean it should affect the approach you have for the next shot. Drop another ball (somewhere without a huge tree in your way, of course), take a deep breath and make a good swing.

The missed shots, the regrets and the times you could've done better? They're in the past. If you dwell on them, you're only setting yourself up to repeat the same mistakes. The key is to *learn* from them and make the necessary adjustments. If you don't, that approach shot ends up in the greenside bunker.

"Until we have finally accepted the fact that there is nothing we can do to change the past, our feelings of regret and remorse and bitterness will prevent us from designing a better future with the opportunity that is before us today."

Jim Rohn

It's easy to get caught up in thinking about the last time we failed or held onto things that didn't go our way. But by doing so, we're wasting the energy and focus we could use to make our next shot count. It acts like an anchor weighing you down. When we let go of past baggage—whether that's material or emotional—we give ourselves the chance to focus on the present and set ourselves up for a better and brighter future.

Letting Go of Material Attachments

Materialism can feel like a reflex. The marketing industry spends billions and billions of dollars vying for your attention. Social media has algorithms designed to keep you engaged for hours on end, showing you the "ideal" life you should have. We accumulate things in the hopes they'll make us happy, fulfilled or impressive to others. Some people would jokingly call it "retail therapy." Yet, the more we cling to these material possessions, the more we become prisoners to them.

If death teaches us anything, it's that we don't get to take any of it with us. You've never seen a hearse with a U-Haul attached, right? When our time here is over, our stuff doesn't really matter. You can't take it with you! What will matter is the impact we've left behind—how we loved, who we helped along the way and what values we stood for.

Here's where the awareness of mortality becomes a powerful tool for decluttering your life. Once you fully grasp that your time on earth is limited, you naturally begin to detach from things that don't add real value to your relationships, your personal growth or your happiness. That designer handbag, the gold earrings or a brand new car? Sure, they're nice. But are they enhancing your connections with others? Are they contributing to your legacy? Probably not.

There's something incredibly liberating about letting go and purging the excess stuff in your house once or twice a year. It's like hitting the refresh button on your entire existence. You start by clearing out that one drawer of random cords and batteries, and next thing you know, you're tossing out old furniture, clothes you haven't worn in five years and even those weird gifts from distant relatives (you know the ones I'm talking about).

Suddenly, your home isn't just cleaner—it feels lighter. *You feel lighter.* You can actually find something without tearing your house apart. Every item you let go of is one less thing to manage, to maintain or to worry about.

Time spent gathering material things—like the "perfect" car, the designer bag or the latest iPhone—often leads to dissatisfaction. But experiences like travelling the world, teaching your kid how to throw a football, spending quality time with loved ones, or even savoring a quiet morning reading a book and sipping a nice cup of coffee offer lasting happiness. They become a part of who we are and they add to the legacy you'll leave behind. They are shaping our memories and perspectives in ways that possessions never could.

It's not that owning things is inherently bad. We all need certain comforts in life. I'm not suggesting you never buy a new outfit or replace your car when necessary—even with a nice car if you can afford it. But it's essential to balance that with a focus on meaningful experiences. When you let go of the mindset that more stuff (or more status) equals more happiness, you make room for the moments that truly matter—like that spontaneous road trip or just being present with your family on a lazy Sunday afternoon.

Stop worrying so much

You've likely heard it before: don't waste energy stressing over things beyond your control. Every moment spent dwelling on past mistakes or worrying about what others think takes away from the chance to create an amazing experience in the present.

"Worrying is like paying interest on a debt you don't owe"

Mark Twain

Most of what we worry about never happens. And if it does, it's not nearly as severe as we imagined in our heads. Yet, we allow our minds to get consumed by these hypothetical scenarios. Remember, every second spent stressing over what *might* happen is time stolen from the present, from moments that could be spent making memories, connecting with loved ones, or simply enjoying life.

Let it go.

So, what's the alternative to letting worry take over? Focus on what's happening *now*, in the present moment. You could be savoring a quiet moment of reflection or embarking on a new adventure. But instead, you're tied up in imaginary outcomes. Worrying robs you twice: first, by stealing your peace of mind, and second, by wasting the precious time you have in the present moment.

One of the best ways to combat this is by practicing mindfulness—being present in the moment and letting go of what you can't control. When you realize that worrying won't change the future—or the past—you can shift your energy toward creating experiences and memories that will last a lifetime. Instead of asking, *"What if things go wrong?"* Try asking, *"What amazing things could I be doing right now?"*

Now, I'm not suggesting that you shouldn't plan for the future you want for yourself and your family. That's very different than worrying about the future. Planning requires intention, visualization, hard work and goal setting.

Planning can lead you to a place you want to be. I highly encourage you to visualize and work hard for the future you want. After all, when we think about the legacy we'll leave behind, executing a well-thought-out plan can make it epic!

It's all about making the most of your *real* life instead of living in the imagined future. A future—by the way—that's not guaranteed! Because, let's face it, life is too short to waste on "what ifs." Focus on the present and fill it with what matters most—moments, memories and meaningful relationships.

Releasing Emotional Baggage

I started seeing a therapist a few years ago, and let me tell you, I was a *hot mess*! I mean, I was angry at just about everything—people, situations, traffic lights that turn red for no reason! I had no idea why.

So naturally, my therapist asks me, "Tell me about your upbringing and your relationship with your parents." And I'm like, "Upbringing? Parents? I'm here to talk about why I wanted to karate-chop my co-worker last week!"

Well, turns out that little ol' me was still holding onto anger from my childhood! I was *floored*. I mean, I thought childhood was just a fun blur of Saturday morning cartoons, playing sports every chance I got and asking for snacks every ten minutes.

But after some digging (and by digging, I mean painful self-reflection), I realized I'd been holding onto stuff from *years* ago—stuff I thought I had forgotten. You know, those moments when you didn't get picked for the school team, or when your sibling got away with eating the last cookie and you took the fall? Apparently, those things linger.

It was like my therapist hit me with a "Eureka!" moment. All these decisions I was making and the way I'd react to things, this is how I'd shield myself from getting hurt again—and it all traced back to my childhood.

I'd been living on "emotional autopilot" for years based on old wounds, completely unaware. Through therapy, I came to the life-changing realization that my family members—*drumroll please*—are human, too! Who knew, right? They mess up, I mess up, we *all* mess up. I have news for you, too—your family members—yep, flawed humans. So let it go! Forgive your parents—it's their first try at life too! It's like we're one big group of beautifully flawed beings—and I'm sure you have your quips too :)

"Resentment is like drinking poison and hoping it will kill your enemies."

Nelson Mandela

Here's the thing about grudges, anger and regret: they take up precious space in your mind and in your heart. And who do they hurt? You guessed it—you! Just like the junk drawer in your kitchen, emotional baggage sits there, waiting to trip you up when you least expect it. Worse, it sucks up your emotional energy, which could be spent on building meaningful connections and experiences. That energy is precious. Use it wisely.

Learning to let go of that baggage is liberating. By forgiving others—and forgiving ourselves—we reclaim the energy we've been wasting on negative feelings. And it's not just about "being the bigger person." Letting go of resentment is an act of self-care. It's about choosing your peace over your pettiness.

One technique for releasing anger and resentment is to adopt a mindset of compassion. Ask yourself, "What if this person who wronged me was doing the best they could with the tools they had at the time?"

This doesn't excuse their harmful behavior, but it can help soften the sharp edges of your pain. They are flawed humans, too. The act of forgiveness isn't for the other person—*it's for you*. It's a decision to no longer let that baggage dictate your life. If my experience holds any weight, forgiving the people who have wronged you will be the best decision you've ever made for yourself.

For me, therapy is like a lifelong subscription to a personal upgrade system. I'm in it for the long haul! It gives me clarity, compassion for others and a much-needed reality check every now and then. Without it, I'd still be out here trying to solve life's problems with the emotional toolkit of a moody teenager.

Embracing Simplicity

Letting go of material attachments and emotional baggage naturally leads us to a lifestyle that's a lot simpler and more focused. Simplicity isn't about living in a sterile, white room with one chair and a plant. It's about stripping away the excess—both physical and mental—so you can focus on what truly matters.

The less stuff you own, the less stuff you have to worry about. This gives you more time and energy to focus on what really matters to you—like meaningful relationships, personal growth, staying healthy or actually enjoying your free time.

Instead of worrying about organizing, decluttering and maintaining an endless list of material possessions, imagine being able to spend your time fully engaged in life. Less stuff means less stress. And less stress means more space—mentally and emotionally—for the things that truly matter.

It isn't just about chucking half your closet or finally admitting that you don't need six different spatulas—though, let's be honest, you probably don't. It's also about decluttering your mind and your calendar.

Have you ever noticed how your phone slows down when you've got too many apps running? That's your brain when you say "yes" to everything. It's time to hit the metaphorical 'force quit' on commitments that don't align with your values.

We've all been guilty of things we don't want to do. "Hey, wanna join our book club where we read the *500-page history of sea turtles*? No? Oh, come on, it'll be fun!" And somehow, you find yourself there, pretending to be interested in the lifespan of turtles while all you really want is to be at home, feet up, eating popcorn.

But when you start saying "no" to those obligations that drain your energy, you're creating space for the stuff that truly makes your life richer. It's like clearing out your garage. Once you've tossed out that rusty old lawnmower, you've got room for... well, whatever makes you happy—maybe a yoga mat or a pool table, or just space to breathe.

The same goes for your time. When you start saying "no" to unnecessary commitments, you open up space for the important things, like catching up with old friends, learning a new skill (or a fun hobby), or finally watching that Netflix series you've been hearing about for months.

Minimalism isn't about living with nothing—it's about creating space for what matters. So, declutter your life, your calendar, and your mind. Say no to the stuff that doesn't align with who you want to be, and watch how much lighter and more focused you feel.

Final Thoughts

The real power in letting go—whether it's material possessions or emotional baggage—lies in the space it creates. When you're no longer tethered to things that don't serve you, you're free to focus on what matters most. This creates a life with more depth, more joy and more meaning.

Letting go is about living with intention and purpose, and it's one of the most powerful steps you can take toward living a fulfilled life. We're all carrying around something we'd be better off letting go of. It might be that extra car in the driveway you never drive, or it might be the grudge you've been holding onto for years. Whatever it is, know that you have the power to release it.

Finally, let's take a moment to envision your grand finale: your funeral. All your loved ones are gathered and they're trying to decide if they should laugh, cry or awkwardly shuffle their feet. Even those people you held grudges against are there in an attempt to be the bigger person.

So, what do you want everyone to say about you?

"Oh, he was the guy who hoarded all those novelty coffee mugs and never let go of his grudge against the neighbor who parked in front of his house!" *Cue the eye rolls.* If that's the highlight of your life, you might want to rethink your priorities. What you really want is for them to reminisce about how deeply you lived, loved and let go of all that petty stuff.

Life is short—don't waste it clinging to grudges or accumulating stuff that only adds weight to your existence. Instead, fill your days with laughter, love and maybe a little bit of spontaneity.

"The average human lifespan is absurdly, terrifyingly, insultingly short."

Oliver Burkeman

Your Legacy

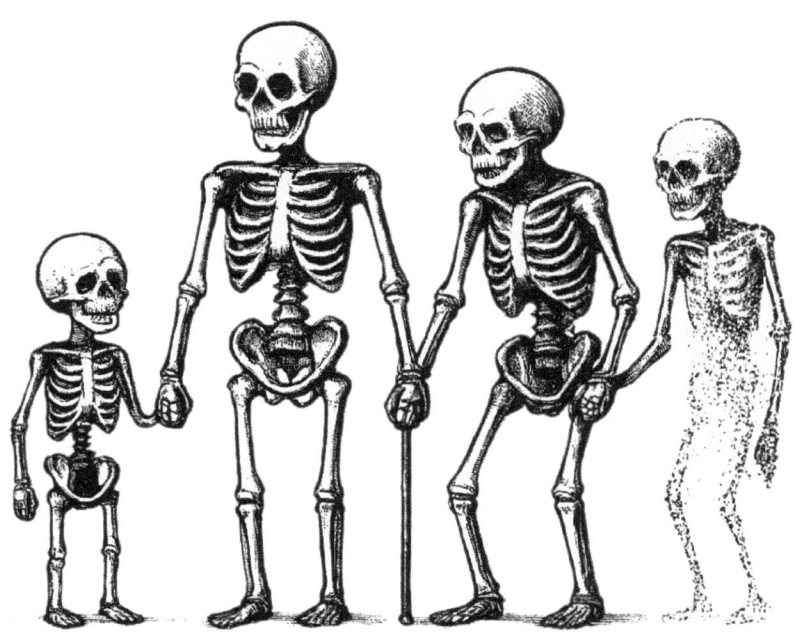

The purest form of love is revealed through your legacy.

Your legacy is meant to invoke a feeling. After you're gone, every thought of you serves as a gentle reminder of what you meant to them and how you made them feel. Your legacy is your grand finale! Your gift to your family and to the world. It acts as a bridge for your descendants, connecting them to your morals and values. Leaving a legacy isn't just about what you leave behind—it's about how you live your life today.

Your legacy might be as simple as the lessons you've taught your children, the positive impact you've had on your community or the relationships you've nurtured over time. Perhaps your legacy is about making your friends laugh so hard they snort soda out of their noses, creating a memory that will last longer than that questionable haircut you had in high school.

In the end, whether you're teaching your kids to ride a bike, organizing that annual potluck where everyone brings a dish they've Googled at the last minute or simply being the person who always remembers everyone's birthdays—your legacy is a tapestry woven from all those delightful and silly moments that make life truly special.

On a personal note, after my friend's passing last year, I found myself reflecting deeply on my own legacy. I was having trouble figuring out where to start. So, after some time, I decided to start writing letters to my daughter—just small stories about her and our family, and little pieces of advice and reflections on life's meaning. It's something I plan to continue as life unfolds, knowing she won't read them until I'm gone. It's a therapeutic process for me and there's real peace in knowing I'll be able to communicate with her clearly, even after I'm no longer here.

Now, I get it—most of us don't go through life actively thinking, "What kind of legacy am I leaving behind?" Most people are too busy trying to keep up with life to give it any meaningful thought. But here's the harsh truth about your legacy— whether you're actively planning for it or not, <u>you're creating it anyway</u>. Everyone leaves some sort of legacy—you don't get a choice in the matter. Some legacies are shit; others are inspiring. Pick one.

It's not just about how people will remember you—though that's a huge part of it—but also about the impact you'll leave that lasts far beyond your time here. Every interaction, every moment of kindness and every moral and principle you live by creates a ripple effect that touches others in ways you will never see.

That's the paradox about your legacy—you work your entire life to create a legacy of meaning and purpose, yet you'll never know the impact it has on others. That's the beauty of it.

So, in this final theme, we will explore some practical—and some crazy—ideas to help you create a legacy of your own. The unique legacy that nobody else on this planet can give. It's your unique gift to the world you leave behind.

Make them proud of you.

Your legacy awaits.

Chapter 10
Your Search for Purpose

"Don't explain your philosophy. Embody it."

Epictetus

We actually die twice.

The first death is the one everyone knows about. The shockwave makes its rounds through your family and social circles. Disbelief and grief hit people like a tidal wave. The funeral arrangements are made, the phone calls come in and the "my condolences" and "I'm sorry for your loss" fill your mailbox and your inbox.

This first death is met with many tears, heartfelt messages and reflections of who you were and what you meant to people. Your immediate family is looking through old pictures and there is an immediate need to celebrate you and the life you've led for all those years. People get dressed up in their nicest clothes, flowers are purchased and the funeral procession eventually makes its way to your final resting place. It really is a beautiful celebration of you and the people in attendance were the ones that always mattered most.

Your second death is quiet. It's not met with flowers, heartfelt messages or funeral processions. Nobody is in attendance for this one. Your second death is the moment—years later— when your name is no longer on the lips of those who attended your funeral. This death doesn't have a definitive date. It just happens naturally over time. As people move on with their lives, your memory recedes into the background and you become another brick in the foundation of their lives.

The way you live your life today and the legacy that you build right now can push back that second death. Heck, there are names we still speak of hundreds of years after their death. Your legacy can be so strong that it becomes impossible not to continue speaking about you after you're gone. When thinking about your second death, make it your mission to find your true purpose and leave a lasting impact on those you love while you still have the opportunity.

————————————————

We live in a turbo-charged, blink and you'll miss it, world. The older I get, the faster it flies by. Your phone is buzzing so much it's auditioning to be a massage chair, your friends are low-key offended you haven't "liked" their 18 Instagram selfies featuring the same coffee cup and you're somehow still trying to keep up with the elusive "Joneses." (Seriously, who are they, and why are they so good at life?) The truth is, at the end of your life, none of this actually matters. I'm being 100% serious. I repeat—none of it matters—*It's all temporary.*

When we slow down (*Pause here. Take a breath*) and really reflect on life and its meaning—AND we look at it through the lens of being mortal—we should be asking ourselves what it really means to live with purpose. I mean YOUR purpose. Not your sisters, your friends or your idols. Yours.

Ask yourself: What meaningful impact can I have on this world? When am I most happy? When am I most proud of myself? Who am I doing all of this for? These are questions worth your time and attention. It's a pathway to finding your own 'why.'

There are no right or wrong answers here, by the way. We're all unique. Some people might say the purpose of life is to chase your dreams. Others might say it's simply about getting out of bed in the morning without hitting the snooze button three times. Either way, there's no one-size-fits-all answer—*and maybe that's the beauty of it.*

Take a moment and give it some thought. Living with purpose doesn't have to mean you've discovered the cure for deadly diseases or solved world hunger. It's personal and unique to you. Purpose can be found in big goals—like running a marathon or achieving an ambitious goal. Purpose can also be found in the smaller, everyday victories—like making a loved one laugh, acing that homemade lasagna recipe or being the go-to person in your group chat for memes.

Purpose can be as grand or as simple as you make it. But here's the kicker—it needs to align with *your* values, not someone else's. So take a second, grab a cup of coffee (or tea, no judgment), and think about what gives your life meaning. Whether it's building a successful career, creating art, performing show tunes in front of your family or mastering the fine art of parallel parking, your purpose is for you alone. It's not for anybody else. Your purpose is what makes you feel fulfilled.

And if you're still not sure, don't worry; you've got time to figure it out. We will go through some great prompting questions at the end of this chapter. Just keep moving forward, stay curious, and maybe—just maybe—stop stressing over having the perfect answer.

Now, stop reading here. Go get a cup of tea :)

———-------------

For me, the idea of living a life with purpose has evolved and morphed over time. I never really thought about it at all in my teenage years. It was about my social circle, having lots of friends (real friends, by the way—not the 'friends' we collect on social media. I'm still very close with my core group of guys), getting my driver's licence as soon as humanly possible and having just enough money by Friday to grab a six-pack of beer to go to the party. Oh, and I also took pride in being good at sports. That was it. Simple.

As life moved forward and I became a husband and a father, my purpose evolved. I began to feel the weight that comes with true responsibility—like real adult responsibility. My purpose morphed into providing for my family, offering my best self to them daily and providing the life, vision and lessons for my daughter to thrive. I love taking care of my girls. They're my why.

More recently, my purpose has morphed into a mortal mindset—contemplating my own mortality and leaving a lasting legacy for my wife and daughter. A legacy that aligns with the morals and values I've adopted along the way. Hopefully, it's a legacy I can pass on to my grandchildren one day.

The bottom line—I want them all to be proud of me.

As I write this book, my purpose is deeply connected to the lessons I learned from my grandfather as a young boy. He lived his life with purpose, even when times were tough. He never lost sight of what mattered—his family, his resilience and his values. His life was a clear example of aligning actions with values and focusing on what truly mattered to him. I've realized that this book is a way for me to extend his second death further into the future. We're not done talking about him yet!

I now put a lot of time and effort into my own "legacy files." It's a series of letters, quotes, instructions, passwords, etc, that my wife and daughter can access once I'm gone. I'm also focusing more on giving back to my friends, my family and my community in hopes of making the lives of people around me a little bit better. I'll elaborate further on these at the end of the book. I'm not saying it's the perfect way of doing things, but it works for me right now—and your job is to discover what works for you.

Let's do an activity: Take a minute to think about a mentor in your life. Try to visualize this person. They can be living or dead. Think of a person who inspires you. What do you think of this person when it comes to their values, their perspectives and living life with purpose?

You have this person in your head?

Check out the PDF on our website to help you through his exercise.

Now—try to break down the characteristics of that mentor. Are they engaging? Witty? Smart? Fashionable? Always on time? What is it they say or do that makes you admire them? Take a minute to visualize them. Are they a good listener? Charismatic in front of a crowd? Write these down!

Your mission: after writing down all of these amazing things about your mentor, have a close look at them and try to emulate those characteristics in your own life. It's that simple. Make the decision to actively shape who you are to become the sum of all the people you admire.

If that mentor is still with us, reach out to that person—have another conversation with meaning and depth. Write down a few questions that are on your mind.

Carve out some time in your calendar and have the conversation! Trust me—they'll be delighted you want to tap into their experience, and you'll never regret the time you spent with them. If your mentor has passed on, the greatest gift you can give that person is trying to emulate their characteristics and living your life by the lessons they taught you. They'll be proud of you.

Living purposefully means being intentional in your decisions, staying true to yourself and making sure you're headed in a direction that fills your life with meaning. Every decision you make must align with the direction you want to go in life. Your decisions must make the 'future you' proud of the 'current you.'

"To my hero. That's who I chase. It's me in 10 years.

Every day, every week, every month, and every year in my life, my hero is always 10 years away.

I'm never gonna be my own hero. I'm not gonna attain that. I know, I'm not!

That's just fine with me because that keeps me with somebody to keep on chasing."

Matthew McConaughey

Purposeful living can be as simple as committing to being a good friend, making others laugh when they need it most or lending a hand to a person in need. Take action in your own life. Think about small changes you could make on a daily basis to live with more purpose. Calling a friend on your way home from work, helping out your parents as they age or something as simple as holding the door for people.

Writing this book is my way of living with purpose. I may not be changing the world, but I'm sharing something I deeply believe in—helping people develop a good relationship with their mortality, live their lives intentionally and create a legacy for the people they love.

As I said before, sometimes life has a way of happening to you! Throwing you a curveball when you're expecting a fastball down the middle—making you look foolish. Attending the funeral of my friend last year was one of those profound moments for me. It hit me hard! It was raw and emotional. I had to start looking at things from a different lens. Immediately.

This is how I align my actions with my values. I'm not trying to write the next bestseller (though, hey, I wouldn't mind), but I'm committed to offering perspective, guidance and a few laughs along the way. Organizing my thoughts within the pages of this book has been therapeutic in so many ways and I hope it helps you with your journey!

Ultimately, living with purpose is about being true to yourself. The key is to figure out what makes you feel fulfilled and build your life around that, just like my grandfather did. It's not about the size of the impact but the depth of your commitment to living a life aligned with your values.

"It's never too late to be what you might have been."

George Eliot

Find Your "Why"

Now, here comes the fun part of finding your purpose—figuring out your "why." Why do you get out of bed in the morning? Why do you do what you do? Why is it all worth it? It's like peeling an onion, except instead of making you cry, it gives you clarity and perspective—though, let's be honest, digging deep might bring a few tears.

This is your chance to reflect on what matters most to YOU. This is unique to you and you alone! Think of the people in your life that matter most to you. What feeling do you want to invoke in them when they think of you?

Simon Sinek's concept of starting with "why" was a game-changer for me. It applies not just to individuals but to entire organizations. The idea is simple: companies that deeply understand *why* they do what they do—beyond profits—are more likely to succeed and inspire loyalty. The same applies to your life. Understanding your why will allow you the clarity to complete the "how" with ease.

In *Start with Why*, Simon Sinek highlights how successful companies lead with their purpose, not just their products. Take Apple, for example. Their "why" isn't simply about selling computers or iPhones; it's about challenging the status quo and encouraging creativity. Steve Jobs understood that this purpose is what attracts such a dedicated following because they resonate with Apple's mission to think differently. Every product they create and every customer interaction is infused with this core belief. Now, the "Apple Army" looks at you like you have three heads when you tell them you own an Android.

Starbucks doesn't just sell coffee. Their purpose is to create a space where people can feel a sense of belonging and connection. Their "why" is rooted in building a community—a place between work and home where people can relax, meet up and enjoy meaningful experiences and exchanges. The wifi signal is always on point at Starbucks to accommodate those breakfast meetings. This deeper mission helps Starbucks foster a loyal customer base that goes beyond a "venti latte, half sweet, triple pump with a full whip" (whatever that means) and overpriced croissants.

These companies demonstrate that when you lead with purpose, it resonates with people on a deeper level. The "what" and the "how" fall naturally into place when the "why" is at the forefront.

The same applies to your personal journey—finding your "why" will help you navigate life with clarity and focus, ensuring that everything you do is aligned with your morals and values. It creates a foundation for meaningful success, not just in work but in life.

Whether your purpose is grand or small, finding your "why" will inspire you to live with intention and authenticity, just like the most successful companies and individuals who have found theirs. Finding your "why" can feel like a journey, but it's one worth taking because it brings clarity, focus and direction to your life. It's your compass. It helps you align your actions with what truly matters to you and it brings you one step closer to your vision.

Note - there is a downloadable PDF on our website to help you navigate and discover your own why. Here's a few pointers on how to start:

Who will be holding your hand?

Think back to that profound scene of you taking your last breath. Who will be there, holding your hand, telling you they love you? These people are your 'why.' These are the core people you should be focusing on. They are the root of your tree. They are the ones who will tell the stories about you after you're gone.

Sahil Bloom refers to these people as your "front row people" in his book, *The 5 Types of Wealth,*

"Close your eyes and imagine you're at your funeral. People are walking in, they're hugging each other, they're crying, and then they all sit down. Look at the front row at your funeral, and visualize the faces of the people that you see sitting in that front row. Those are your front-row people."

I absolutely love this concept of your 'front-row people,' and if you want anyone to be proud of you after you die—it's them.

What activities make me feel alive and energized?

Think about what excites you, whether it's helping others, being creative, public speaking, solving problems or leading a team. Your passion often points toward your purpose. If you're having trouble finding this within yourself, start trying new things that are outside your comfort zone. Challenging yourself in this way can trigger a renewed sense of purpose. Seriously, change it up and try something new.

When do I feel most proud of myself?

Reflect on moments when you felt accomplished, whether it was something big like completing a project, having a great workout or comforting a friend. Maybe you overcame your fear of public speaking and received compliments after you were done. These moments of accomplishment reveal what brings you joy and satisfaction. Now, go ahead and chase that feeling over and over. Go for it!

What would I do if money were no object?

Imagine your ideal day or career if financial constraints didn't exist. What would you spend your time on? This question strips away external pressures and gets to the heart of what truly makes you happy. We all get busy in the hustle and bustle of life, the "rat race," as many call it. We need to realize that money is nothing short of a 'tool.' It's essential—no doubt. But it's not at the core of our purpose. If we strip away those financial pressures, what is it that brings you joy and fulfillment?

Identify Your Core Values

Alright, time to dig deep and ask yourself the big questions. What are the principles that guide your life? Are you all about honesty, creativity and compassion? Or are you a thrill-seeker who lives for adventure? Are you an introvert that loves your quiet time or do you thrive in social settings? Write down your top five values (don't worry, this isn't a school test—there are no wrong answers).

These values are the foundation of your purpose. Think of them as the ingredients in a recipe. You wouldn't bake a cake without flour, right? Well, you won't find your purpose without identifying the core values that drive you! If you're stuck, ask a close friend or family member to help you out. They'd be happy to share what they see in you.

Think of words like integrity, passion, honesty, resilience, compassion, empathy, gratitude, loyalty, generosity, mindfulness, courage, and humility. Make your own list. What are the top values that define who you are? Write down your top five.

Look for Patterns

Now that you've got your values, it's time to play detective. Look at the answers and see if any patterns start to emerge. Maybe you light up when you're helping others, or perhaps you're happiest when you're exploring new ideas. These little breadcrumbs are leading you straight to your "why." It's like solving a mystery, but instead of discovering who ate the last slice of pizza, you're discovering what makes *you* tick.

Write Your Purpose Statement

Here's where it all comes together. Once you've gathered your thoughts and found those patterns, try summarizing your purpose in a single sentence. Don't panic; you don't have to make it sound like the title of a blockbuster movie!

Something simple like, "My purpose is to inspire others through creativity and bring joy through storytelling," or, "My purpose is to help people live healthier, more fulfilled lives," works perfectly. Maybe you find joy in helping your community, "My purpose is to bring value to my community through charity work." This purpose statement will serve as your life's compass, helping you make decisions, set goals and learn to embody the vision you've created for yourself.

Just remember: your purpose statement should *feel* right. It doesn't need to impress anyone else. It's your life, your story, and you're the author!

It is important to understand that your purpose statement isn't something you carve into a stone tablet and place on your mantel forever. It's a flexible "working document" and should evolve with you as you experience life. It's more like a favorite pair of shoes—comfortable but subject to change as your life evolves—and maybe a little scuffed up along the way. It grows with you and adapts to new experiences like mine did when our daughter came into the picture.

Before she arrived, I thought my purpose was crystal clear— work hard, build a career, maybe travel a little and find time to relax. Then *bam*—fatherhood! Suddenly, my purpose shifted from just self-focus to nurturing, teaching and preparing her for a meaningful life. Now, my daily purpose is filled with things like writing letters to her for when I'm gone, creating a legacy of lessons and love, and making sure she knows how to fold a fitted bed sheet (still working on that one).

The key is to *test* your purpose in real life. Does it still feel right? Does it still get you out of bed in the morning? If it's not quite hitting the mark, don't panic. Adjust it. Like life, purpose is an ongoing process of discovery, and what feels perfect now might shift again later. Maybe next year, my purpose will involve building the world's most organized garage (wishful thinking).

The point is that living with purpose isn't a straight line—it's more like a road trip with lots of detours and pit stops (and maybe some engine trouble), and that's what makes it exciting. Keep testing, adjusting and evolving with each new chapter of your life.

Live It Out

Now that you've identified your "why" and you've put together some type of compass for yourself, the final step is to integrate it into your daily life. Set intentions that align with your purpose, make decisions based on it and prioritize activities that support it. Remember—this is a book about recognizing the fleeting nature of life—*time is our most valuable asset*. It's not money or possessions. Learn how to use time wisely! Living with purpose will give you a renewed sense of meaning and direction.

"Leading with purpose will bring fulfillment and success in ways that simply focusing on the "what" and "how" never can."

Simon Sinek

Take your time—this isn't a race. It's a lifelong journey of discovery and alignment. By completing this activity to find your purpose, you allow yourself to focus on what makes you tick. The rest of it blurs into the background where it belongs.

Chapter 11
Creating your Legacy

"Legacy is not leaving something for people.

It's leaving something in people."

Peter Strople

Congratulations on getting this far. Seriously. It's no small task to really look yourself in the mirror, drop the ego and accept the fact that you're not that big of a deal in the grand scheme of things. Hey—we're only a tiny speck compared to the size of the galaxy, right? It is what it is. Nothing any of us can do about it.

There is so much power and freedom in acknowledging this fact and living your life to the fullest. And if you've been paying even a 'speck' of attention, you should notice a trend in our little journey together. You're here for a short time, folks! So make it count.

I'm drawn to the story of my grandfather for a number of reasons. Not only does it stem from my admiration for him; but it's also the simplicity of his teachings. The gentle reminders of life's fragility and the priorities he held dear until his final days. His legacy to me is about his awareness—and acceptance—of his mortality. Knowing all along that his life will end no matter what he did about it. Instead, he focused on his 'why.' At the end of the day—or even the end of your life—one question will stand above the rest: *How did you make others feel?*

Imagine your entire life as a movie playing in a full theater, from the time you were born until your final breath. The theater is packed and all the people watching have eyes that are glued to the screen—popcorn in hand. The audience is laughing and crying through all the twists and turns of your story. But, when the credits roll and the audience begins to leave the theater, what feeling will linger in their hearts?

Will it be the image of the car you drove, the designer bag you "had" to have, the stock you bought that 'changed everything' or the collection of baseball cards you couldn't let go of? Or will it be the genuine, heartfelt moments that made them laugh until they cried? The stories you told at bedtime, the laughter that filled your house or the advice you provided to help guide them? Will they feel a genuine connection with you and finally grasp what you stand for? What emotion will they have in their hearts?

In order for the audience in that movie theater to relate to you and your story, you have to be willing to be vulnerable. To forget what the masses tell you about what you *should be* and to just be who you truly are. Let your light shine despite the opinions of others. So when the curtain falls and the theater goes dark, future generations look back with gratitude, cherishing the legacy you left behind and the impact you made on the world. A life so good that once in a while, the kids say, "Hey, mom, can we watch that old movie again about [insert your name here]?"

"Be who you are and be that well."

St. Francis de Sales

Let's dive into the nitty-gritty of creating a legacy that even your future great-grandchildren will brag about—because when they sit around the dinner table, they won't be talking about the stuff you own. They'll be recounting the stories of how you made their world a better place—one awkward family gathering at a time!

Check out the PDF on our website to help guide you through this process.

Defining your legacy is unique to you. It means being true to yourself the entire way and committing yourself to causes that matter to you. Is it your commitment to your family? Your passion for helping others? Your charisma? Making a mark on your community?

This is where your unique abilities come into focus! We all have something special about us—something that makes us uniquely qualified to leave our mark on the world. It's like having a superpower, but instead of wearing spandex and flying through the sky, you're equipped with your quirks, talents and passions.

So, what does that look like in practical terms? It could be anything from your knack for storytelling that makes every family gathering entertaining, your ability to bring out the guitar and carry a tune by the campfire or maybe your uncanny ability to whip up a gourmet meal out of three ingredients. Maybe it's your talent for making people laugh, even when the going gets tough, or your deep empathy that allows you to connect with others on a profound level. Whatever it is, let it shine!

The legacy you leave isn't just about grand gestures or monumental achievements; it's about the everyday actions that reflect your unique gifts. It's the warmth you spread when you help a neighbour or the inspiration you provide when you mentor someone.

"I've learned that people will forget what you said, people will forget what you did, but people will never forget how you made them feel."

Maya Angelou

So, as you think about your own legacy, remember that it's not about waiting for the right moment to unveil your greatness. It's about showing up every day for your purpose and letting your special qualities shine through in your actions. The more you embrace your unique abilities, the brighter your legacy will become. After all, the world needs what only you can give—so don't hold back!

This book is a testament to that notion. I never in a million years thought that I would write a book. Seriously, I grew up as a 'jock' with a mediocre grade in English class. My grade 12 English teacher called me a "legume." I had to look it up.

But here I am, putting my ideas down on paper and sharing them with the world. To be perfectly honest, I have no idea if this book will be embraced or not. But at the end of the day, I'm doing it for my daughter. It gives her something to have after

I'm gone. It gives her guiding principles for living a life with meaning. That makes it totally worth the effort.

Leaving a meaningful legacy doesn't require fame, fortune or earth-shattering achievements. It's often the small, consistent actions that add up over time. Imagine if, every day, you took just one action that aligned with your legacy. Maybe it's helping a colleague navigate some personal challenges, volunteering an hour per week at a local shelter or simply being present for a loved one in need. These seemingly minor acts (to you) can create ripples that extend far beyond your immediate circle. It could mean the world to others.

When you think of legacies, it's easy to imagine the famous figures: Nelson Mandela, Dr. Martin Luther King, Mother Teresa, Amelia Earhart, Steve Jobs, Charles Darwin and even Albert Einstein (I know, I know—just the tip of the iceberg). These giants are often heralded for their monumental contributions to society. However, some of the most powerful legacies come from ordinary people living their lives with purpose—people like you and me.

Take, for example, a local teacher who inspires her students to pursue their dreams, regardless of their backgrounds. Every time she stays late to help a struggling student or advocates for her class, she's shaping not just their futures but the future of the community. Her legacy may not make headlines, but it's a profound testament to the difference one person can make. Think about it: she might be the reason a student believes they can become a doctor instead of just dreaming about it. That's the kind of legacy that sticks around longer than a viral TikTok.

Then, there's the story of a neighbor who regularly bakes cookies for the elderly residents in the area. To her, it might feel like just a simple act of kindness, but to those receiving her treats, it's a reminder that they're loved and valued. Picture little old Mrs. Thompson, sitting alone in her living room watching the Price is Right—suddenly receiving a warm plate of cookies. At that moment, her heart swells, and she feels connected to her community. It may spark a friendship that may have never seen the light of day. The neighbour's legacy of compassion spreads through her actions, creating an interconnected community that fosters belonging and care.

Take the example of the local baseball coach who sacrificed their Saturday mornings for 30 years, teaching the local youth how to throw a strike or hit a line drive up the middle. Their approach to teamwork produces countless adults who pay it forward and pass on the teachings to their kids and neighbourhoods. Hey, maybe the next Derek Jeter is one of those kids!

These examples illustrate that small, everyday actions can carry significant weight. You don't have to launch a global movement or invent the next smartphone to leave a lasting legacy. Sometimes, it's about the little things: lending an ear to a friend in need, sharing your favourite book with someone who's struggling or simply making eye contact and smiling at the cashier.

Remember that the people you encounter are all dealing with their own problems, often invisible to you. A smile in the hallway, a compliment at the coffee shop or a simple "How are you?" can mean more than you might think. We often forget that behind every face is a story, complete with struggles and triumphs.

"Be kind. Always. Everyone you meet is fighting a great battle."

Ian Maclaren

Take a moment to consider this: when was the last time you felt overwhelmed? Perhaps it was juggling deadlines, dealing with family issues, or just trying to figure out how to assemble that IKEA furniture without losing your mind. Now, picture someone offering a kind word or helping hand during that tough time. It's those small acts of kindness that have the power to turn someone's day around.

So, make a conscious effort to be that person who uplifts others. Show compassion and help them see the good in their own life. A compliment, a helping hand or simply being present can be the difference between someone having a good day or a bad one. Remember, small acts of kindness go a long way. You might just inspire someone to pay it forward, creating a chain reaction of goodwill that transforms not just their life but also yours.

Be the light in someone else's life.

So, as you reflect on your own legacy, consider the ordinary moments in your life where you can make a difference. The next time you have the chance to brighten someone's day— through a simple compliment, an act of kindness or a listening ear—seize that opportunity! Because in the grand scheme of things, it's these small acts that build the foundation of a legacy worth leaving behind. One day, someone might share a story about how you made them feel valued, cherished or inspired.

A Practical Guide to Leaving a Legacy

Building a legacy isn't just about the emotional and moral impact you leave behind—it's also about making things easier for your loved ones after you're gone. It may not be the most thrilling task to think about, but proper planning is one of the greatest gifts you can give to your family.

I repeat—building your legacy is the greatest gift your family can receive after you're gone.

The purest form of love is revealed through your legacy.

You don't want to leave them scrambling in a time of grief, trying to figure out your passwords, funeral preferences or where the mortgage papers are. Here's a practical guide to making sure your legacy doesn't just inspire people but also supports those you love in concrete ways.

Full Disclosure: I'm far from an expert in this field. These are merely suggestions. Seek out the right professionals to provide further guidance for you.

Have a Will (And Make Sure Someone Knows About It)

Think of your will as the roadmap for how you want your estate to be handled. Without it, the state could decide who gets what, which can cause delays, probate, family disputes and even financial losses. A proper family ensures that your wishes are respected, from dividing up assets to deciding who will care for your children or pets. Once you've got it all written down, get it notarized by a lawyer. Don't forget to tell your loved ones where they can find it!

Better yet, have multiple copies in different locations—like a safety deposit box or at the lawyer's office. The best will in the world won't do much good if nobody knows it exists.

Identify Powers of Attorney and Executors

Having powers of attorney (POA) in place ensures that someone you trust can make decisions on your behalf if you become incapacitated. There are two main types: medical and financial.

A medical POA can make health care decisions, while a financial POA can manage your assets and debts. Be sure to communicate clearly with your designated POAs so they know their responsibilities and understand your wishes. This can prevent a lot of confusion and hardship later on.

An executor is a trusted person who follows and obeys your wishes (as outlined in your will). They execute these wishes so all of your beneficiaries get what they deserve. Try to pick somebody younger than you that you trust—especially if you're in the later stages of life. It wouldn't hurt to have a backup as well in case they predecease you.

Money and Life Insurance Policies

Leaving behind savings can be one of the greatest gifts to those you care about. For your loved ones, it might mean paying off debts, chasing dreams or finally splurging on that trip to Hawaii. If you're feeling extra generous (or mischievous), include instructions like, "Use this for something epic—no boring bills allowed!" Or perhaps just, "Spend it wisely... and maybe think of me while you're doing it."

Life insurance is another great option for leaving a financial legacy. It can provide your loved ones with the funds they need to cover funeral costs, pay off debts and continue living comfortably after you're gone. The best part? Death benefits from life insurance policies are tax-free! This means your family won't have to worry about a hefty tax bill when they're already dealing with your loss. Make sure your beneficiaries are updated regularly to reflect your wishes and make sure they are aware of these policies. Again, make sure someone knows where it is!

Leave letters, recordings or video messages.

One of the most heartfelt ways to leave a legacy is by writing letters or recording video messages for your loved ones. These messages can provide comfort and guidance long after you're gone. You can share your thoughts, memories and advice. Hey—maybe even record a song! Anything that you believe will help them feel your presence. These letters, recordings or videos are a personal way to remind your loved ones of how much you care for them.

Passwords and Financial Information

In the digital age, much of our lives are protected by passwords—from social media accounts to bank accounts. Make sure to leave behind a secure list of your passwords for critical accounts and financial information. You can use a password manager to securely store them and provide access to your spouse or trusted family members. This ensures they can close accounts, manage finances or handle subscriptions without unnecessary stress.

Funeral Plans and Preferences

Nobody likes thinking about their own funeral, but leaving clear instructions can make a tough time a little easier for your family. Whether you want a traditional service, a celebration of life or even something more unconventional, let your loved ones know.

You can also decide on burial or cremation, music, readings or anything else that will help reflect your life and legacy. This gives your family the peace of mind that they're honouring you in the way you'd want.

By taking the time to plan these things out now, you're saving your family from additional stress during what will already be a challenging time. Not only does this reflect love and care, but it ensures that your legacy continues to support, nurture and guide them in all the ways that truly matter. It's not just about leaving behind stuff—it's about leaving behind peace, clarity and a sense of continued presence. That's a legacy worth building.

Your Legacy Awaits

As you ponder the legacy you want to leave behind, remember that it doesn't have to be perfect. In fact, the beauty of legacy lies in its imperfection. It's about progress, not perfection. The key is to start taking those small, deliberate actions today. Define what matters to you, align your daily choices with those values and watch as your legacy unfolds.

In the end, what will people say at your funeral? Will they talk about how you had a great watch collection or how you made a difference in their lives? By consciously creating your legacy, you ensure that the latter is the story they'll share. So, go ahead—get out there and start crafting a legacy that will outlive you!

Try out our "legacy builder" tools in the downloadable PDF on our website

Chapter 12
The Art (and Fun) of Planning
Your Own Funeral

"Always go to other people's funerals; otherwise they won't come to yours."

Yogi Berra

Nobody wants to think about their own funeral. It's right up there with doing taxes, getting a root canal or listening to your neighbour's "one-man-band" rehearsal. But here's the thing—you don't want your loved ones doing this for you. They'll be grief-stricken, overwhelmed, and, let's be real, probably not in the best state of mind to decide whether you'd prefer a sleek mahogany coffin or to go out in a Viking-style pyre (which, by the way, is still illegal in most places—just so you know).

In this chapter, we're going to make this whole 'death thing' not just palatable but—dare I say—kinda fun. That's right. Planning your own funeral doesn't have to be grim. In fact, it's one of the most caring, thoughtful, and yes, even hilarious things you can do for your loved ones. Think of it as your final act of love...with a side of dark humour.

Undoubtedly, the people attending your funeral will be emotional. Of course, they'll be—after all, you were an amazing human being! The tears will flow, the sniffles will echo and perhaps even a stray wail or two will slip out from the back row.

There is deep beauty in funerals. If you've made a positive impact on people, they'll find a way to be there for you. No matter what they're up to in their life, people you've impacted will move mountains to make sure they are at your funeral to pay their respects. This feeling they experience is a testament to your legacy. But as they express their grief, let's give them something to cry *and* laugh about. Imagine, amidst the tears, you orchestrate one final laugh! That, my friend, is nothing short of a miracle.

Before you bite my head off for being insincere, let's touch on psychology one more time. Laughter is often described as the best medicine, and for good reason. It releases endorphins, the body's natural feel-good chemicals, which help reduce stress and create an overall sense of well-being. Laughter also strengthens social bonds, allowing people to connect more easily with others, especially during difficult times like grief or loss.

Planning your own funeral with a pinch of humour is like giving your loved ones the greatest parting gift possible—the gift of laughter when they least expect it. What a beautiful twist it is to have people leave your service smiling, possibly even chuckling, as they fondly recall the time you wore a tutu to a serious office meeting or how you always told the worst dad jokes at every family gathering.

As the planner of your own farewell party, you get to set the tone. Maybe you want your eulogy to start with, "Well, I guess I'm not running late this time!" Or perhaps you throw in a pre-recorded message like, "Relax, everyone! I'm finally getting that eternal vacation I've been talking about!" Or maybe, "No need to be sad—I've got front-row seats to the best concert of all time up here!"

A little humor can lighten the mood and give your loved ones a playful nudge to remember the good times, even as they're saying goodbye. After all, what better way to remind them that you've just upgraded to the ultimate VIP lounge in the sky?

Humour during a funeral isn't just for the fun of it; it serves a profound purpose. It reminds people of the joy you brought into their lives and creates a light-hearted atmosphere in a time of heaviness. It's almost like you're pulling off one final prank from beyond the grave—keeping your spirit alive by making people giggle right when they thought they couldn't. What a legacy to leave behind!

If you've managed to get everyone to laugh *at your own funeral*, you're officially a legend. Seriously. Plus, who wouldn't want to be remembered as the person who could still crack a joke while being dead?

Now, let's get into the practical side of this crazy idea!

Step 1: Show Me the Money

The average funeral is expensive! When you add up the coffin, the gravestone, the pastor, the flowers and even the little cards people collect at the front door—we're talking a good chunk of change here! It is the kind of money we'd all prefer to spend on a vacation to Italy, a new car or a truly ridiculous hot tub. But when it comes to funerals, that's the cost—unless you're planning on going DIY (and please don't).

Setting aside the funds ensures your family isn't left scrambling to pay for things like flowers, burial plots and whatever else the funeral home will convince them you "would have wanted."

This brings me back to the life insurance piece from earlier. Unless you're swimming in money—or have some secret treasure buried somewhere—life insurance is one of the most practical and thoughtful ways to leave a financial safety net for your loved ones. This money can go a long way in planning and executing your funeral. While it may not be the most thrilling topic to discuss, it's a crucial part of securing your family's future once you're gone. Think of life insurance as a final, grand gesture—a way of saying, "Even in death, I've got your back."

Also, let's be real: leaving behind some funds for your funeral gives you *some* control over how this whole thing will go down. It's your final hurrah—go out in style.

Step 2: To Be or Not to Be (Cremated)

Ah, the great cremation debate. Some people want to be buried, some want to be cremated, and some have wild ideas about being shot into space or turned into a tree (I respect the creativity!). If cremation is your choice, make sure to say so clearly in writing. And if you have special requests for where your ashes should be spread, here's your chance to make it epic—or absurd.

For instance, my dad has this grand idea that he wants his ashes spread on the 12th tee at Augusta National. I'm not sure why. You golf fans will know that it's a stunning par-three hole called "Golden Bell," measuring about 155 yards, where players have to hit over Rae's Creek.

The irony about this particular location is even if he had 10 attempts to land a shot on that iconic green, he'd miss all 10!

And while I love the man, I had to remind him that if I did that, he'd better have an extra $30,000 USD set aside for my bail!

So unless you want your final resting place to involve your kids' mugshots, be reasonable—or at least generous with the bail fund.

Step 3: Organ Donation?

Are you planning to donate your organs?

Don't leave your loved ones playing detective on whether or not you are into organ donation (it's a bit time-sensitive). So mark it down, make it official and let them know you're ready to give the gift of life...even when yours is done.

No judgement here—everyone is different and has the right to choose. But organ donation is one of the most selfless things you can do. It's like the ultimate parting gift: "Here, take my heart—it's in great condition!" Even after you've exited the stage, you're still out there helping people. What a way to go!

I recently came across a powerful story that truly touched my heart. A man who had received a life-saving heart transplant decided to meet the widow of the person who had donated the heart. After some time had passed, the widow had the chance to use a stethoscope and listen to the beating heart of her deceased spouse—still alive in another body. What an emotional and special moment it must have been to hear the echo of her loved one still beating on, giving someone else a chance at life.

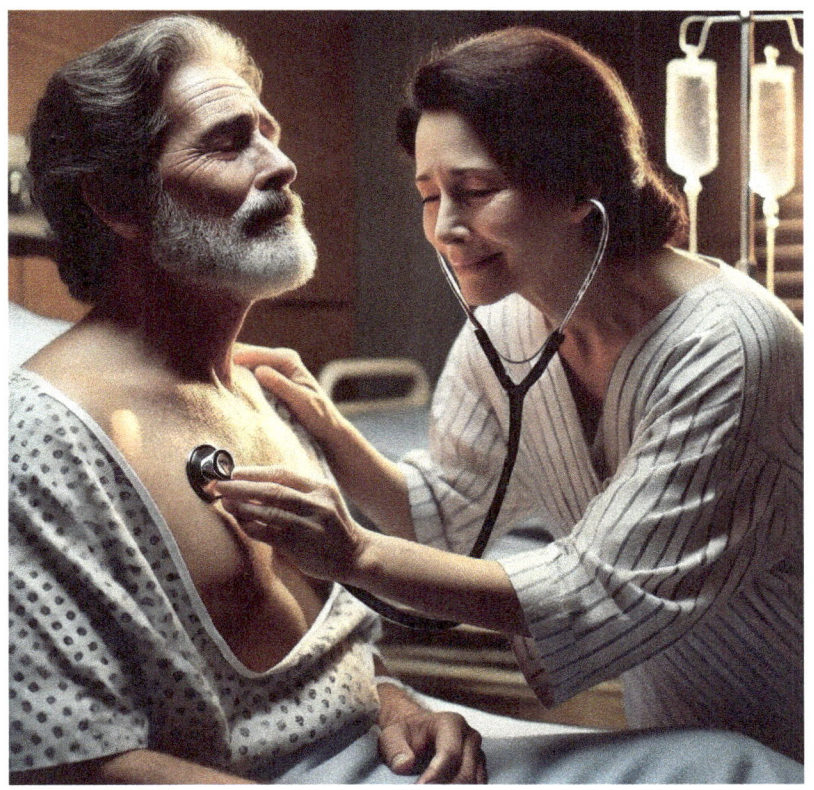

It's a reminder of the extraordinary gift organ donation can be. Not only does it save lives, but it also provides comfort to the grieving, knowing that part of their loved one is still out there, helping others live fully.

It's a testament to the legacy we can leave behind, one that goes beyond ourselves, bringing light to others even in the darkest of times. Imagine the gratitude the recipient must have felt, not only for the second chance at life but for the connection to the person who made it all possible. Moments like this help remind us of the beauty in selflessness and the ways our lives can continue to ripple outward even after we're gone.

Step 4: Have you lost the plot?

No, I'm not talking about a Netflix series—I'm talking about a *literal* plot of land! If cremation isn't your thing, or maybe you're feeling undecided (half-cremated, half-buried? You do you—no judgment!), securing your final resting place early is a huge win for your family! It's like buying your last bit of real estate—except you won't have to worry about mowing the lawn. Trust me, you'll save your loved ones so much stress by just owning that tiny, eternal slice of the Earth. It's like the gift that keeps on giving.

Even *dead* people aren't escaping the real estate market. Prices are only going up, even in the afterlife! So, locking down a plot now is kind of like investing in the world's most exclusive gated community—except the only fees are flowers and maybe the occasional visit from your in-laws. So go ahead, claim your land, and secure your forever home.

Step 5: Special Instructions (Make It Fun!)

This is where you can really get creative. Do you want to be buried with your lucky poker chips? Maybe you'd like a Viking helmet placed on your casket (again, it's still not legal to burn it, but the helmet? Is totally doable). Do you want the hearse to play "Highway to Hell" as it pulls into the cemetery? No problem.

Or maybe you're like my father, with dreams of a scenic golf course. While I can't promise to fulfill his exact wishes, I *do* love the idea of leaving special instructions that leave people laughing through their tears. Maybe have a confetti cannon go off at the end of the service or have a life-size cardboard cutout of you waving people out the door. Nothing says "I loved you all," like leaving behind a good gag.

Be specific. Do you want a celebration of life with a photo montage set to Celine Dion's greatest hits? Or a casual backyard BBQ with a keg and a playlist that screams, "I have great taste in music"? These details matter!

Listen, I'm not here to downplay the seriousness of your funeral—people will be sad, of course. There will be tears, tissues and heartfelt sobs. Your family, close friends and loved ones will be devastated—because, obviously, you were awesome! But here's the thing: with a little forethought and planning, you hold the power to make your farewell just a little less gloom and doom and more celebration of you. In fact, adding personal touches that make people smile—maybe even laugh for a brief moment—can be a beautiful reminder of how you lived your life and how you want to be remembered.

Think of your funeral as your final performance—a chance to share your sense of humour, your wit or your warmth one last time. Maybe it's in the form of that quirky playlist that perfectly captures your personality or perhaps it's a well-timed, pre-recorded video message where you kick off with, "Well, folks, I finally made it! It's gorgeous up here!" These little details can bring levity in the midst of heartache and serve as a fitting tribute to the person you were—someone who knew how to make people laugh, even when things were tough.

Isn't that how you want to be remembered? As someone who didn't just leave an empty hole in people's hearts but also filled it with joy, laughter and a good story or two? You've got the power to plan it your way—a send-off that reflects your spirit, your humor and your unique approach to life (and death).

Step 6: The Last Word: Your Funeral Speech

Here's your chance to make your funeral truly personal. Whether you want to leave a heartfelt goodbye or a hilarious "I told you so," writing your own funeral speech is a fantastic way to be part of the event—without actually being there.

Not into writing? No problem—record a video. You can give your loved ones some final wisdom, like "Don't sweat the small stuff" or "Make sure the life insurance policy is in the top drawer." Or just crack a few jokes: "If you're watching this, I guess things didn't go as planned."

Your funeral is the last great celebration of you, and with a little planning, you can make sure it's one that brings more smiles than tears. Sure, people will cry—they're going to miss you—but with a little effort on your part, they'll also remember you with a laugh, a smile and maybe even a confetti cannon.

Start planning the most *you* funeral anyone's ever seen. Because, let's face it, death may be inevitable, but a boring funeral? That's optional. Think of it as your last big project, but without any deadlines (pun intended).

Follow along with the downloadable PDF on our website

Chapter 13
Joe

Earlier in the book, I told you about a dear friend who passed away from cancer. He was far too young, 42. What I didn't share was just how deeply his passing rocked my world. I didn't expect to be as emotional as I was, tears streaming down my face uncontrollably. His funeral wasn't just a time to grieve; it was a wake-up call that made me look at my own life in a whole new way.

He had a daughter the same age as mine. As I stood there at his Celebration of Life, the parallels between our lives were undeniable and overwhelming. It's time to fully honour him by name. His name was Joe.

Joe's death wasn't just the loss of a friend; it felt intensely personal in ways I hadn't expected. Standing at his funeral, I couldn't stop thinking about his wife and daughter and how they would face the future without him in it. I found myself wondering about all the milestones he would miss—graduations, walking his daughter down the aisle at her wedding and those everyday moments we sometimes take for granted.

At that moment, I couldn't help but think about my own daughter. What if it had been me? What would she do? What memories would she have of me after I was gone? The thought hit me like a tsunami. It catapulted me into hyperdrive to get my shit together!

Joe wasn't just someone battling an illness; he was a father, a husband, a son, a brother and a friend. A 'normal' guy trying to juggle life while making the most of his time spent with the people he loved. Joe's story felt so relatable because it could have easily been mine. *It could have been anyone.* His passing made me question everything I thought I had time for—time with my family, time with my daughter, time to nurture relationships, time to forgive and live a life that truly matters.

Your time on earth is finite.

I often smile when I think back about the last time I saw Joe. It was at a family swimming event—one of those rare, perfect days when a dozen of my buddies and their families rented a local pool just to enjoy life together. Joe showed up that day—unexpectedly. I was jumping in and out of the pool, playing with the kids, soaking wet. Then, I suddenly saw him sitting there through the window, smiling at all the chaos. Kids were splashing around, and more water was out of the pool than was in it.

Joe was in and out of the hospital for over a year at this point, and the treatment was taking a toll. Seeing him was emotional for me. I wasn't expecting it. I cried when I saw him, not sure if I'd ever get the chance again. We were getting regular updates on our group chat from some close friends, and we all knew it was serious. But there he was, sitting by the pool, smiling, looking like he had summoned every bit of strength just to be there with us. I put my fist against the window, a tear pouring down my face (he never knew it was a tear; I was wet from the pool). He met my fist with his own, smiling at me and giving me a quick wink through the glass.

Joe wasn't just physically present that day—he was truly there in spirit. He made sure to talk to everyone, telling us he was feeling better. But there was something profoundly different.

His voice was deeper—raspier—not the sound we were used to. And yet, his energy was undeniable. There was a calmness about him, almost like he had found peace with his situation. It wasn't small talk, either—he was engaged, making sure everyone felt his love and his presence.

Joe and I had one of those conversations that will stick with me forever. We talked about life, about the people we love, and, of course, we talked about our daughters. His pride and joy was his daughter. Joe's eyes lit up whenever he spoke about her, and you could hear the love in every word. The last thing Joe said to me before he left that day was, "It's all about time with the people I love."

When Joe left the swimming event that day, I had a feeling it might be the last time I'd see him. At the time, I pushed that thought aside, wanting to believe he was getting better. But later, I realized he wasn't just visiting that day—he was saying goodbye.

And in hindsight, there was something quietly beautiful about it. Joe knew his time was limited, but he chose to spend his remaining days in the best way possible: with the people who mattered most to him, leaving an impact that would live beyond his time here on Earth.

Four months after seeing Joe at the swimming pool, he passed away in the hospital.

Joe and I had a bond that went beyond casual friendship—we didn't see each other often, but when we did, it was meaningful. We could talk about anything, from the serious to the ridiculous. He was always there to listen, always willing to lend a hand to anyone who needed it. Joe had this rare gift of making everyone feel like they mattered, no matter what he was going through.

As I listened to his wife speak at the Celebration of Life, she shared a touching story about Joe that warmed my heart and brought a smile to my face. One afternoon, they had plans to meet in the city, where they relied on public transit. The plan was to meet at Union Station, but Joe didn't show up at the time they agreed. She called him—no answer. She tried again—still no answer.

Later, she discovered that Joe had gotten sidetracked. He'd been walking along to meet his wife when an elderly woman fell down and seemed a bit injured. Joe helped this woman and was completely absorbed in offering her support. Unaware of the passing time. He was focused on who was in front of him. That's what Joe's legacy is. Being present in the moment and always willing to lend a hand.

Joe and I shared a fun little joke about our hair. See, both of us started turning grey—excuse me, silver—around the same time, and rather than complain about it, we embraced it. We called ourselves the "Silver Foxes."

It was our little "club," and we loved the humor in it. But let me tell you, Joe always rocked that silver mane better than I did. His hair was so stylish it was almost *unfair*. I used to joke that he should have been on the cover of a magazine. He had that effortlessly perfect haircut that made the rest of us look like we'd just rolled out of bed. Joe would laugh it off, but man, did he always look sharp!

But underneath the humor and the Silver Fox jokes was a deeper connection. It wasn't just about the hair; it was about how he navigated life's twists and turns. He always made people feel important—always present, always giving, no matter what.

I decided to call his wife to discuss more about Joe. To gain a better understanding of who he really was. She shared with me the charities and initiatives he was passionate about. She shared stories about how he volunteered his time to help special needs children learn how to ski. She shared that, despite his diagnosis, he always made the doctors and nurses at the cancer center laugh and feel welcome in his presence.

We've included links and descriptions to Joe's favorite charities on our website.

At Joe's funeral, I witnessed just how many lives he had touched. Friends, family, his beloved daughter—they were all there; the place was packed! All of them mourning the loss of a man who had shown up for them in ways that truly mattered. Joe wasn't wealthy in the traditional sense, but he was rich beyond measure when it came to relationships. And standing there, listening to people share stories about him, I realized something profound: It's not about how much time we have, but how we spend it and who we spend it with. Joe got that, and it was clear that he had lived his life by that truth.

Joe's passing left a lasting mark on me, one that I hope resonates with you as well. We all know a Joe. His life is a powerful reminder that time is our most valuable asset. More than money, more than success, more than the things we chase every day. It's the moments we spend with the people we love that truly matter. We often think we have all the time in the world, but Joe's story shows us that's not the case. Any one of us could find ourselves in his shoes. Tomorrow is never guaranteed.

Joe's life, especially in those final months, is a shining example for all of us. He didn't shy away from his fate—he embraced the time he had and made it meaningful. His legacy is a testament to living fully, loving deeply and never taking time for granted. Joe didn't wait for the "perfect moment" or for life to be ideal. He showed up, even when it was hard, and poured his heart into the people around him. That's the legacy he left behind, and it's one we should all strive for.

So, if there's one lesson you take away from this book, let it be this: *Time is our most precious asset. The relationships you nurture with those you love and the impact you have on others will become your true legacy.*

So, don't wait. Speak the words that matter. Maintain perspective. Take risks. Cherish every moment with the people you love. Embrace life with open arms and live it fully. Life is fragile, and time slips away faster than we realize. Joe understood this, and he filled his final days with love, kindness and grace. That is the legacy he leaves behind—a reminder that our time is precious.

Now, the question is yours to answer: how will you choose to fill the remaining squares on your 52x90 grid?

Your legacy awaits.

Good Timber

by Douglas Malloch

(Joe's favorite poem)

The tree that never had to fight
For sun and sky and air and light,
But stood out in the open plain
And always got its share of rain,
Never became a forest king
But lived and died a scrubby thing.

The man who never had to toil
To gain and farm his patch of soil,
Who never had to win his share
Of sun and sky and light and air,
Never became a manly man
But lived and died as he began.

Good timber does not grow with ease,
The stronger wind, the stronger trees,
The further sky, the greater length,
The more the storm, the more the strength.
By sun and cold, by rain and snow,
In trees and men good timbers grow.

Where thickest lies the forest growth
We find the patriarchs of both.
And they hold counsel with the stars
Whose broken branches show the scars
Of many winds and much of strife.
This is the common law of life.

Afterword

I want to sincerely thank you for joining me on this journey. It's not easy leaning into who you truly are and being honest with that person in the mirror. I sincerely hope you were able to take something from this book and apply it to your own life.

Writing is brand new to me. I never grew up thinking that this would become a part of my journey. I'm glad it has. It has been an extremely rewarding experience and It's a testament to my newfound purpose.

I didn't share with you the answers my father gave me with those ten questions. It was a wonderful exercise to get to know him on a deeper level. To this day, I'm still not sure who got more out of the exercise: him or me.

As I mentioned earlier in the book, he was hesitant at first, but he was clearly touched by the thought of me wanting to get to know him on a deeper level. After reading his answers, I realized how much he loved his family and how he endured many of life's challenges along the way.

Note - these answers are unedited.

What were some of the greatest experiences in your life?

➤ Watching the birth of my four children

➤ Holding my grandchildren for the first time

➤ Seeing my children all become amazing adults and parents

What experiences would you still like to have before you die?

➢ Make a real and positive difference in the life of someone I don't know.

➢ Become a Great-Grandfather

➢ Create some kind of process where I can "give back" to others who are less fortunate

What "little things" do you enjoy most in life today?

➢ Being able to do what I want to do when I want to do it

➢ Watching my grandkids grow and improve at everything they do (sports, academics, learning right from wrong, maturing, I can keep going)

What do you realize now that you took for granted when you were younger?

I took for granted that I was talented enough to get where I wanted to go without having to work hard at it. I was very wrong. It was a valuable lesson.

What things did you love doing as a kid that you never talked about?

➢ Anything to do with sports. Sports was always my "happy place"

➢ Most people don't know that I was a yo-yo champion. Lol.

What big goals or dreams did you have when you were young?

When I was young, all my dreams centred around sports. Professional hockey player was number one. Habs, of course. Also wanted to be independently rich, not because of the money but so I could follow any road that interested me without worry.

What advice would you give me now that you haven't been able to tell me yet?

You will be faced with many decisions throughout life. Always lean toward the decision that will bring you and your family the most happiness. Remember, money is usually not the number one thing that brings the most personal enjoyment, rewards or happiness. Be true to your beliefs.

What are your biggest regrets in life?

I had trouble with this one. After thinking through regrets and after giving them enough thought, I could only conclude that almost every regret actually led to something more rewarding that would not have happened if I had not experienced the regret in the first place.

➤ Not being able to go to university after high school forced me to do it at night while working and raising a family...a much more rewarding experience.

➤ Refusing a transfer at work led me to be laid off. But that led to a fulfilling career at another company that lasted almost 30 years.

I do have one regret that I still struggle with—deciding to move my mother into a home when her health was beginning to fail. To this day, I blame myself for not taking her in with us and figuring it out. She was not happy in her final years.

If you could go back in time and change just ONE thing in your life, what would it be?

Taking my mother in for her final years. It was hard to watch her

If you could put a sign on a billboard to tell the world ONE message - what would it be? And why?

I would actually want two billboards.

One - You're here for a short time. Leave it all on the field.

Two - Your word is all you have. Be true to it.

This exercise with my father was both a bonding experience and a chance to learn who he was and what made him tick all those years. As I mentioned before, when you ask a mentor for their insights and expertise, they light up like a Christmas tree! He was smiling just as brightly as those days under the pile of wrapping on Christmas morning.

I encourage each of you to reach out to special people in your lives. Find out what makes them tick. Ask them questions about life, about love and about legacy.

Your time is now. Go for it.

The Mortal Mind Reading List

I realize that I covered a number of deep and meaningful concepts throughout this book. The truth is, I've only scratched the surface. Much of what I've learned comes from the pages of the books listed below. These authors have inspired me, challenged my thinking, and shaped my perspective on life, death and everything in between.

This reading list isn't about adding more books to your shelf—it's about gaining insights that will help you live with more purpose and intention. Take what serves you, leave what doesn't and apply what you learn.

On Mortality & Meaning

Briefly Perfectly Human – Alua Arthur

A death doula's perspective on embracing mortality as a gateway to living more authentically.

How to Die – Seneca

A philosophical reminder that death is the final, inevitable chapter—so we'd better do it well.

Meditations – Marcus Aurelius

The ultimate Stoic handbook on accepting death, living with virtue, and making peace with impermanence.

Tuesdays with Morrie – Mitch Albom

A reminder that life is short, love matters, and our legacy is built on relationships, not achievements.

4000 Weeks - Oliver Burkeman

A poignant reminder about the finite nature of life

On Living with Purpose

Start with Why – Simon Sinek

If you don't know your "why," you're just running in circles. Find your purpose before time runs out.

Who Will Cry When You Die? – Robin Sharma

Life lessons to help you live meaningfully and leave a lasting impact.

The Monk Who Sold His Ferrari - Robin Sharma

Embracing simplicity to find meaning in life.

The Four Agreements – Don Miguel Ruiz

Four simple yet profound principles for living with integrity, clarity, and purpose.

The Alchemist – Paulo Coelho

A fable about following your dreams and embracing the unknown—because, in the end, the journey is all we have.

The Happiness Advantage - Shawn Achor

People believe you need to be successful in order to be happy. In fact, the opposite is true: focus on your happiness and success becomes inevitable.

On Mindset & Growth

The Obstacle Is the Way – Ryan Holiday

Challenges aren't roadblocks—they're the path forward.

Ego Is the Enemy – Ryan Holiday

Success isn't about feeding your ego—it's about humility, learning, and constantly evolving.

Stillness Is the Key – Ryan Holiday

In a noisy world, clarity comes from cultivating stillness and embracing presence.

Discipline Is Destiny – Ryan Holiday

Self-mastery is the foundation of a meaningful life. The habits you build today shape your future.

Courage Is Calling – Ryan Holiday

Fear will always be there—but courage is the choice to act despite it.

The Subtle Art of Not Giving a F*ck – Mark Manson

Time is limited, so choose your battles wisely.

The Diary of a CEO - Steven Bartlett

Profound lessons on business, success, mindset, and personal growth.

Greenlights - Matthew McConaughey

Greenlights are moments of opportunity—when life flows smoothly. Red and yellow lights (challenges, setbacks) eventually turn green when viewed in hindsight.

On Wealth Beyond Money

The 5 Types of Wealth – Sahil Bloom

True wealth isn't just financial—it's time, health, relationships, and fulfillment.

The Gap and the Gain – Dan Sullivan & Ben Hardy

Stop measuring yourself against an impossible future—appreciate how far you've already come.

Who Not How – Dan Sullivan & Ben Hardy

Focus on what only you can do. Delegate the rest because time is your most valuable asset.

The 10X Mentor – Grant Cardone

You can 10X your income, but not your lifespan. Prioritize accordingly and think big!

On Reinvention & Letting Go

Do Over – Jon Acuff

You can restart your career, but not your heartbeat. Don't wait until it's too late.

*Unf*ck Yourself* – Gary John Bishop

Overthinking is a waste of time, and time is running out. Take action now.

Level Up – Rob Dial

Life is a game, and you don't get extra lives. Play at your highest level every day.

The Let Them Theory – Mel Robbins

Let them misunderstand you. Let them judge. You have better things to do with your time.

The Warrior Within – John Little

Bruce Lee's philosophy on flowing with life instead of resisting the inevitable.

These books are just the beginning of my journey of self discovery. It is my hope that these suggestions are just the beginning of yours as well.

Thank you,

Michael

Joe's Charity Work

Throughout Joe's battle with cancer, he was deeply touched by the mission of a remarkable charity: **Nankind**. In his honor, we invite you to learn about this organization and consider supporting them through a donation link under Joe's name available on our website.

Visit our website to learn more

www.themortalmind.com

Nankind is dedicated to easing the challenges faced by families when a parent is diagnosed with cancer. Founded in 2009 by Audrey Guth during her own cancer journey, Nankind provides free services such as childcare, counseling support and meal programs. Their goal is to help children build emotional resilience while allowing parents time to rest and focus on their recovery.

To date, Nankind has supported over 2,200 families, empowered more than 4,000 children, delivered 65,000 meals, and provided 40,000 hours of free childcare.

www.nankind.com

Supporting this charity not only honors Joe's commitment but also extends a helping hand to countless families navigating the complexities of cancer. We encourage you to visit **themortalmind.com**, where you'll find a donation link to Nankind.

Your generosity, in any amount, can make a significant difference in the lives of those Nankind serves. Thank you for your consideration. Continue to live your remaining days, making an impact on those around you.

With Gratitude,

Michael